THE SAVVY ADVENTURE TRAVELER

WHAT TO KNOW BEFORE YOU GO

ELLEN DUDLEY

Camden, Maine • New York • San Francisco • Washington, D.C. • Auckland • Bogotá • Caracas • Lisbon • London
Madrid • Mexico City • Milan • Montréal • New Delhi • San Juan • Singapore • Sydney • Tokyo • Toronto

Ragged Mountain Press
A Division of The McGraw-Hill Companies

10 9 8 7 6 5 4 3 2 1

Copyright © 1999 by Ellen Dudley

Photo credits: Pages 1, 43, 111, 117, 138, and 145 by Ellen Dudley.
Pages 13 and 74 by Eric Seaborg. Pages 27 and 58 by Scott Darsney.
Page 84 by Sam Carlson/*Backpacker* Magazine. Page 125 by Ellen Dudley/Eric Seaborg.

Library of Congress Cataloging-in-Publication Data
Dudley, Ellen, 1938-
The savvy adventure traveler : what to know before you go / Ellen Dudley
p.   cm.
Includes index.
ISBN 0-07-018013-X (pbk.)
1. Travel—Guidebooks.   I. Title
G153.D84   1998
910' .2'02—dc21   98-29343
CIP

Questions regarding the content of this
book should be addressed to:
Ragged Mountain Press
P.O. Box 220
Camden, ME 04843
www.raggedmountainpress.com

Questions regarding the ordering of this
book should be addressed to:
The McGraw-Hill Companies
Customer Service Department
P.O. Box 547
Blacklick, OH 43004
Retail customers: 1-800-262-4729
Bookstores: 1-800-722-4726

♻ This book is printed on 60-pound
Renew Opaque Vellum, an acid-free paper
that contains 50 percent recycled waste
paper (preconsumer) and 10 percent post-
consumer waste paper.

Printed by R.R. Donnelley & Sons
    Crawfordsville, IN
Design by Eugenie Delaney
Production by Deborah Krampf;
    Ðan Kirchoff
Edited by Gerald Novesky;
    Kathryn Mallien

CONTENTS

ACKNOWLEDGMENTS

MY HEARTFELT THANKS TO ALL THOSE WHO SHARED THEIR STORIES, advice, and background information: adventure travelers, foreign outfitters, and staffs of adventure travel companies.

My deep appreciation to the two busy doctors who reviewed the medical section: William B. Cobb, M.D., Consultant, Epidemiology and Infectious Diseases, St. Mary's Hospital, Grand Junction, Colorado; Scott Luria, M.D., Associate Professor, Internal Medicine, University of Vermont College of Medicine, Burlington, Vermont.

And special thanks to my eagle-eyed editor-in-residence, Eric Seaborg.

INTRODUCTION

PADDLING UP THE AMAZON, TREKKING IN THE HIMALAYAS, BICYCLING through Vietnam . . . not so long ago such adventures were the exclusive province of intrepid explorers who were not only young and restless, but also bold and experienced. But today anyone who's reasonably fit—teenagers to golden agers—can leave the civilized world behind for an active, exciting journey into the heart of an exotic land.

And they can leave not only the driving but the planning and logistics to the experts. Adventure travel companies provide leaders, schedules, food, shelter, and transportation for group journeys to some of the most remote and exhilarating landscapes, and some of the most fascinating cultures, on earth.

These adventure travel companies produce slick, seductive catalogs describing their destinations and itineraries, with trips to suit a wide range of vacationers—professionals, retirees, singles, and families. Their lush color photos depict ordinary people in exotic settings having the time of their lives. And most adventure travelers do come back saying, "That was the most incredible trip I've ever taken."

But adventure travel involves a lot more than checking into a luxury resort or hopping aboard a tour bus. Traveling in any backcountry area is complicated and risky, and venturing deep into developing countries amplifies these risks enormously. Standard tours baby their clients but adventure travel companies expect a certain level of self-reliance. You need travel savvy and wilderness skills to make a successful switch from armchair to outback.

Company brochures say, "Expect the unexpected." That's why they call it *adventure* travel—you never know for sure what you're getting yourself into. Even with an experienced, well-paid guide, things can go wrong.

To stay safe and comfortable you must know how to choose the right trip and the right company, how to get ready, what to take, how to stay healthy, and how to avoid the problems that can ruin this vacation of a lifetime. And your travel agent, your doctor, and your adventure travel company can't tell you everything you need to know.

This book will outline the vital steps you need to take to avoid problems and have a safe trip and a good time. It's an all-in-one how-to guide for adventure travelers—a step-by-step practical handbook full of tips, strategies, checklists, and advice spiced with tales of lessons learned the hard way.

CHAPTER 1

THE TIME OF YOUR LIFE

THIS IS LION COUNTRY," THE NATIVE TANZANIAN GUIDE explained as the group prepared to bed down in their sleeping bags. "If you have to get up during the night, don't stray more than three feet from your tent. Just in case we get a visitor."

As the adventure travelers drifted off to sleep, they could hear a pride of lions roaring not far away, answered by another pride in the distance. The campers were up in the gray light before dawn for tea and toast before venturing forth across the Serengeti veldt to seek a lion kill. Not far away, two of the big cats were so engrossed in feeding on a wildebeest carcass, they scarcely noticed as the truck crept close enough for the travelers to snap pictures.

Until recently, a safari like this was a privilege reserved for a select few. If you had dreams of following in the footsteps of Marco

1

Polo or Dr. Livingstone you needed the brawn and bravado—not to mention the time and fortune—to mount a lengthy and daring expedition. A journey to a remote part of the world was something you experienced vicariously by reading a travel narrative or attending a lecture.

With the boom in the adventure travel industry, such trips are now within reach of anyone willing to take a chance and make the commitment. Today, if you're reasonably fit you can follow the Silk Road or the Inca Trail for about the same amount of time and money you'd spend on a cruise or resort vacation. Adventure travel companies offer a tantalizing array of exotic destinations with all the logistics organized for you—including itineraries, food, shelter, and transportation. They supply the guides as well: experts who take you deep into the wild—and bring you back out again.

Adventure travel is the fastest-growing segment of the booming leisure travel market. Millions of people are taking these trips, but many of them are leaving home without the proper knowledge or preparation. They don't realize that at some point they might need to fend for themselves—that even the largest adventure travel companies can run into trouble despite their expertise and experience.

Consider the group basking in the surreal midnight sunlight on cliffs above the Arctic Ocean, toasting their arrival at the "top of Europe." They were relaxing at the midway point of a six-hour round-trip night hike across the tundra, a highlight of a Scandinavian adventure travel excursion. For their midnight buffet, their guide had brought an ambrosian picnic in his knapsack: fruit, Swiss chocolates, and cloudberry liqueur. The night was idyllic—until they began their return trek across the undulating expanse to their van. A thick fog suddenly extinguished the pale sun and within minutes reduced their visibility to a three-foot circle within a damp, cold cloud. Nothing to worry about, however, they thought as they stumbled along blindly, following their guide across the trackless landscape—after all, they'd each paid this reputable adventure travel company $200 per day to safely lead them through dicey conditions.

But as the minutes turned to hours, no road emerged from the mist. Some of the hikers—experienced outdoorspeople—had brought emergency gear and were prepared for the sudden damp cold, but others became soaked and chilled. Two hikers began to shiver convulsively—a first sign of potentially fatal hypothermia. Finally the leader admitted the unthinkable: He was lost. He'd remembered the sumptuous treats but had forgotten his compass, and in the dense fog they had probably been wandering in circles.

The group huddled together on the lee side of a boulder to discuss their predicament. One woman had a suggestion. She had noticed that the wind had been off the ocean, blowing on her right cheek as they had walked west from the road to the cliff. If they could keep that breeze on their *left* cheeks now, they could parallel the ocean again and eventually reach the road. It worked—within an hour they'd found the van and were headed for hot showers.

Those adventurers returned with little more than an exciting story to tell, but their experience shows that even in a developed country such as Norway adventure travel calls for more skills and preparation than the average vacation.

A few in that group knew you should toss rain gear into your daypack—even on a clear evening—but the others didn't realize you should always be ready for a sudden reverse in weather fortunes. And no one in the group had brought a compass. Adventure travel companies don't include that little gadget on their lists of items to bring—after all, they supply the guide whose job it is to find the way. But a compass is one of those "never leave home without one" items that adventure travelers should always carry.

Thousands of people are signing up for rugged trips these days, to far riskier places than Norway, blindly trusting their company to take care of them even in the most primitive jungles and deserts. They leave the safe confines of home without the skills and gear they might need in an emergency. Most merely pay some price in discomfort; some return with injuries or illnesses that could have been prevented; and, sad to say, occasionally some never return.

Adventure travel companies offer trips to all the continents. You can paddle the Amazon, trek to Everest, hop onto Antarctic ice floes, photograph the Serengeti, hike an Inca trail, sleep in the Sahara, dance with Balinese firewalkers, camp with Indian camel traders, snorkel with Galapagos sea lions, and mingle with reindeer in Lapland.

But before you choose one of these trips, you need to know if it's the right one for you. Before you commit a large sum of money, you need to know how to check up on the company you're entrusting yourself to. And before you go, you need to prepare—for months ahead in some cases—in order to stay healthy and make the most of your trip.

WHAT IS ADVENTURE TRAVEL?

FOR MOST PEOPLE, THE MENTION OF A TOUR GROUP CON-jures visions of the "If this is Tuesday it must be Belgium" holiday. On a conventional sightseeing package tour, a bus disgorges a horde of tourists at a standard point of interest. They're expected to view it within the assigned time frame—whether it's the Louvre, the Uffizi, or the Taj Mahal—and get back on the bus to be whisked away to the next temple of tourism.

The typical hop-on-and-off-the-bus tour features crowds of people straining to hear cookie-cutter descriptive spiels at the "must-see" sites. At the end of the day, the bus deposits everyone at a hotel with rooms that are Hiltonized for American tastes and dinners that are de-spiced for American palates. On many of these trips you might see all the cultural sites but miss the culture altogether.

Adventure travel trips are quite different. They generally feature physical exertion, exotic locales, and primitive logistics. Most of these trips are based on hiking, some on bicycling or paddling. Others require less exertion but traverse exotic third world locations that most travelers would find too difficult or intimidating to visit on their own.

More than likely when you do find yourself in a vehicle, it will be a small, rugged one. If you do bed down with a roof over your head, it will be a native lodge or indigenous hotel. And although you might stop at the main tourist spots, they'll be just a prelude to the path-less-traveled, back-of-beyond places only adventurous travelers manage to see.

Another key difference between adventure travel and standard tours is the adventure traveler's deep immersion in an exotic society and landscape. On the typical adventure travel trip you venture into a remote region, leaving behind the neon, the concrete, and many of the comforts of civilization—and you absorb a strange culture in a way you never could on a "standard" tour.

Having few luxuries actually breaks down the barriers between you and the sights, sounds, and smells of the world you've traveled so far to experience. The physical exertion—the act of getting out into nature under your own power—also sharpens your powers of observation, strengthens your bond to the land, and increases your appreciation of your surroundings.

GET OFF THE BUS, GUS

If you stay on that air-conditioned bus, you'll never walk down a dusty road, exchanging greetings with Berber women washing their djellabas by the village well.

If you bed down in an air-conditioned hotel, you'll never wake to the howls of baboons or the cries of macaws.

If you travel with a pack of fifty fellow tourists, you'll never visit a Masai chieftain in his mud hut.

If you eat in the tourist-route restaurants, you'll never taste goat goulash and pigeon pie.

And if you'd just as soon pass on experiences such as these, you're not a likely candidate for adventure travel. If a cold martini before dinner and a hot shower before bed are vacation requirements, you should stick to standard tours in the civilized world.

Adventure travel isn't a hedonist's dream trip. Club Med it's not. You need to be able to trade the soft, easy, familiar life for one that might be lumpy, rocky, and smelly.

On a moderate adventure travel trip you won't need thunder thighs and bulging biceps, but you will need the right attitude. Delays and discomfort are the norm. You just need to be able to go with the flow, take in the scene, maintain a calm stoicism. In short, the happy and successful adventure traveler is curious and flexible, tolerant and good natured.

If you'll forego some comforts to get off the beaten path, you'll find incredible rewards. And you'll understand why so many adventure travelers return home saying, "I had the time of my life." Your memories will last forever, many of them more relaxing than a meditation mantra. Replaying scenes from the Sahara or the Serengeti will drop your workaday stress levels faster than a bear market drops the Dow.

There's one thing you probably won't bring home: extra pounds. On the active trips, most people actually lose a few. On a rigorous mountain trek you can chow down 5,000 calories a day and still come home lighter, not to mention stronger and healthier.

LONG AND RUGGED TO SHORT AND SOFT:
SOMETHING FOR (ALMOST) EVERYONE

Adventure travel companies cater to an increasingly wide range of interests, ages, and abilities, offering a range of trips, from long and rigorous to short and soft. You can take a month-long trek over 17,000-foot passes in the Himalayas or a ten-day photo safari in a Land Rover.

Companies grade their trips from "easy" to "extremely rigorous." Because baby boomers are aging and seniors are more active today, many companies are designing easier itineraries, with "soft" adventures to complement their longer treks and rugged floats. Nowadays you don't have to say good-bye to all the creature comforts when you sign up for one of these trips.

The "softer" trips—such as photographic safaris, bird-watching, elephant-riding, and four-wheel-drive tours—usually offer cushier accommodations. There's generally a correlation between exertion and amenities: The easier the trip, the greater the number of luxuries.

Many trips feature stays in lodges, but even on camping trips surprising touches have been introduced. For instance, in the midst of the African bush, your campsite could feature a tented bathroom with porcelain fixtures, hot showers, and odor-reducing chemical toilets. You might eat in a dining tent at a table complete with cloth and napkins. And you might retire to a "cabin-style" stand-up-inside tent with cot and linens. You might find other "civilized" aids as well, such as special outlets on your safari vehicle for recharging your video recorder.

On "tougher" trips, you'll eat seated on the ground, crawl into a tent, and bed down in a sleeping bag on a foam pad. Bathroom facilities might include wash basins and a tented pit latrine—but on some treks they just issue a do-it-yourself trowel.

When you begin contemplating a trip, it's best to read the catalog descriptions carefully and pay attention to the terminology: An adventure travel company's "rustic hut" in Borneo doesn't mean the same thing as a realtor's "cozy cabin" in the Catskills.

You'll also need to consider your tolerances, both physical and mental. Even some young and fit athletes suffer from altitude sickness, and some city slickers just can't abide primitive conditions. It's up to you how daring—or cautious—you want to be.

But here's one point to bear in mind: On almost any adventure travel trip, some of the amenities will be either missing or "interesting." The infrastructure will be more primitive, the logistics more complicated, the culture more unpredictable, the weather more extreme, the transportation more iffy.

THE "ACTIVE" ASPECT

The physical activities featured in many adventure travel trips aren't meant to be athletic competitions. Hiking, paddling, and bicycling are means to an end. When your own muscle power gets you out in the open, under the sky, away from the vehicular cocoons of steel that insulate you from the land and the people, you absorb so much more.

When you travel in a slow, exposed manner, you notice intriguing details and encounter native people along the way. Many say the best way to see any country is on foot; in fact, that's often the *only* way to reach some remote regions.

But even if you're hiking far into the hinterlands, chances are you won't have to heft the thirty-plus pounds of clothing, sleeping bag, food, cooking pots, stove, and other equipment you'd normally have to carry yourself. "Trekking" means not having to carry your own gear: Porters or pack animals will do the heavy lifting for you. You'll only need to carry a light day-pack with an extra layer of clothing, your camera, and your water. But you'll still get to experience the joys of wilderness backpacking and sleeping under the stars.

On less physically demanding trips, you might sample an intriguing variety of conveyance options—maybe a safari truck or river raft plus a camel ride across the desert or an elephant ride through the jungle. Even if you opt to ride, be prepared to get just as wet or dusty as you would on foot—and perhaps even saddle sore as well!

A TYPICAL TRIP

The typical trip is a jam-packed ten days to two weeks, tailored to meet the needs of those with demanding careers who can get away for only a limited time.

The typical difficulty level is "moderate," with a blend of physical activities and cultural exchanges. Like all adventure travel trips, the daily accommodations, itinerary, and virtually all the meals are prearranged and included in the trip price.

Usually you'll travel on your own to an international airport at your destination country where you'll be met and transferred by minibus to your first night's lodging. Typically, your room will be in a small hotel that reflects the country's culture. You won't wake up and wonder whether you're in Cuzco or Chicago.

When you check in you'll receive instructions about meeting for dinner and an orientation meeting. Your group will be small—usually somewhere between eight and fifteen. The trip leader will go over your itinerary in detail and answer any questions.

You might spend the next day or so touring this gateway city; then you'll take off on a domestic flight, train, or van to the starting point for your journey.

The next morning you'll meet the group for breakfast and then set off with just your daypack—some water, an extra layer of clothing, and your camera. Your duffel—with all the rest of your belongings—will be transported for you.

You'll be up early, often by 6:30 A.M. You'll walk for three or four hours, then stop for a leisurely lunch prepared by the staff. You'll have a little time afterward to rest or catch up on your journal. In the afternoon you'll walk for two to three more hours and get into camp by midafternoon. Tents and such will be set up already and the staff will have dinner simmering on the camp stoves.

Some companies offer budget, do-it-yourself trips. For these you trade a lower cost for more effort on your part: You'll set up your own tent and take turns with communal chores such as cooking and dishwashing.

WHO GOES ON THESE TRIPS?

In the early years of adventure travel companies, about the only choices offered were rigorous mountain climbing or risky whitewater rafting. Most participants were in their twenties or thirties, in peak physical condition, and able to get away for a month-long expedition.

Today, baby boomers and just-retireds fill most of the slots on adventure travel trips that are half as long and far less demanding. The average adventure traveler is between forty and fifty years old, a busy professional with disposable income (but little time), looking for an exhilarating, exotic, challenging vacation with all the details taken care of in advance. This traveler is educated (often with an advanced degree), affluent, and ready to spend at least $3,000 on this vacation.

In response to the increase in "softer" trips, more families and retirees are signing up. Women of all ages are a big segment of the adventure travel market, often attracted by the safety-in-numbers aspect. And singles of both sexes who can't pry a friend away from hot showers and a soft bed are attracted to these trips because they supply ready-made companions. In fact, some companies report that half their groups are made up of people who sign on without knowing anyone else on the trip. These solo travelers often form lifelong friendships with their adventure travel cohorts.

Some catalogs list "singles only" trips as well as special trips for women, seniors, and families.

The activity and its degree of difficulty will shape your group's composition to some extent. Most of those on a strenuous, high-altitude trek will be in their thirties and forties—but you're likely to find a couple of fit sixty-year-olds as well.

Most adventure travel companies blend physically active exploration with wildlife sightings, cultural sightseeing, and people-to-people exchanges. But there are all sorts of unique itineraries designed for special interests: birding, wildlife, diving, photography, mountaineering, and volunteer mini–Peace Corps experiences.

For instance, if you're a birder and you need to spot the yellow-rumped cacique and the ruddy-breasted seedeater to complete your life list, you could sign on with an expert ornithologist leading a trip to a prime refuge at nesting time. If you're a camera buff, you could join a group led by a professional photographer who will dispense advice on exposure and depth of field just when you need it—when you're out in the bush and want to capture a Cibachrome moment.

HOW MUCH WILL IT COST—AND WHAT WILL YOU GET FOR YOUR MONEY?

TRIPS USUALLY COST BETWEEN $2,000 AND $3,000 OR more, not including your international flight. But this money can save you a lot of time and eliminate a lot of grief. The adventure travel company has researched all the details in advance and will solve myriad problems for you.

If you've traveled independently in Europe you know it's usually easy to find food, shelter, and transportation to the next town, even if you don't know more than twenty words of the language. So you might think, "I could manage one of these trips on my own, for a lot less money." And maybe you could. But chances are you never could sandwich one of those back-of-beyond, third world itineraries into your two-week vacation—or even come close.

Your travel agent could arrange a lovely itinerary for a European sojourn—a series of charming *pensions* linked by train—with the precision of a Swiss watch. But setting up—and guaranteeing—arrangements in developing countries is dicey and difficult. Third world transportation systems can be crowded and unreliable. For example, flights often are overbooked, or canceled, or depart erratically. Deciphering the timetables and systems—and actually fighting your way on board—can be difficult tasks that can take days when you're traveling alone. And many destinations involve a complicated transportation itinerary: boats, buses, trains, small planes, four-wheel-drive vehicles, maybe even a pack train.

Then there's the monumental problem of finding your way to the sights in those remote regions—picking the best route, then getting permits and a reliable guide. At some national parks and game preserves you might find yourself on the outside looking in if you go it alone: Many such places limit the number of entry permits, and tours often get priority. And you'll be days away from a U.S. consulate if anything really bad happens—such as serious illness or tribal warfare.

Adventure travel trips are like expeditions: They require enormous amounts of advance planning and local knowledge to organize the logistics so that your trip leader can move you along without a hitch, so you don't lose hours (or days) waiting for the guide at the temple, lunch at the cave, the permit at the national park. The companies have local staff who know the language and know how to do business from baksheesh to bribery. In essence, you're hiring a micromanager and staff so you're spared the headaches that go with figuring out and nailing down all the mundane details that will ensure a smooth trip. It's the "leave the driving to us" concept that frees you from all the hassles. No worries about finding and cooking your food, finding someone who speaks English, or setting up and taking down your camp; you're free to enjoy and absorb your experiences, with spare time to relax, write postcards, take photos, write in your journal, or reflect on the miraculous day you just had.

WHY YOU NEED TO BE CAREFUL
WHEN CHOOSING YOUR COMPANY

The catalogs are enticing and glossy, like coffee-table books; they're filled with the romance, beauty, and adventure of it all. The sun is always shining, the natives always friendly. Everyone is relaxed and healthy, having a wonderful time. And the advertisements are glowing. One featuring African trips promises: "It's safe . . . it's exciting . . ."

The degree to which your trip will match those images and claims depends to a great extent on the travel company you choose. Some companies will schedule trips only in prime seasons; others run trips in the shoulder of the peak season, and even off season, when it could be chilly or rainy. Some companies run trips to countries on current "dangerous places" lists—where there are insurgencies, bandits, and terrorist attacks on tourists. After all, the most interesting destinations are the least developed—and often the least stable.

Some of these companies have the experience and contacts to keep you out of trouble in unstable regions. Others don't, such as the one with the driver who led his group into fatal trouble: He ventured into rebel territory; guerrillas sprayed his passengers with automatic-weapon fire.

Some companies know how to find the most reliable transportation. Many third world conveyances are iffy—planes without instruments, trucks without brakes. But the better companies will minimize these risks by contracting with outfits that supply safer vehicles, newer planes, saner drivers, and better pilots.

Most companies refer to the dangerous aspects of adventure travel in the back of their catalogs in fine print. Generally, they include clauses absolving them of responsibility and liability for injuries and damages including everything from acts of God to the all-encompassing "force majeure." Not that they don't warn you. As one company notes: "Before you agree to undertake a holiday in a wild or remote area, you should clearly understand that besides discomfort it might involve you in personal risk."

WEIGHING THE RISKS AND REWARDS

Any trip involves risks, and if you want to pare them down to a bare minimum you should stick to standard resorts that provide safe and predictable food, lodging, and activities.

However, if last year's traditional vacation left you somewhat bored and dissatisfied, rested but not energized, pampered but not exhilarated, you might be ready to try the ultimate escape—an adventure travel trip. Sure, there will be more risks, but you can minimize them by choosing your activities, your destination—and your travel company—very carefully.

CHAPTER 2

THE RIGHT TRIP AT THE RIGHT TIME

A DVENTURE TRAVELERS SHOP IN CATALOGS, BROWSING through colorful pages filled with appealing destinations. But making a smart travel purchase is a lot more complicated than choosing the style and color of an outfit. To pick the trip that's right for you, you need to do some careful research and comparison shopping.

Choosing a destination is easy. The rest is trickier. You need to pick a trip that's right for you, one that matches your interests, physical abilities, and bank account. Moreover—*and this is extremely important*—you need to choose the right adventure travel company.

WHERE TO GO

YOU MIGHT WANT TO VISIT A COUNTRY WHERE YOU'VE never been, an exotic land you've always dreamed of seeing; or you might choose one where you've been before, but as a tourist, not a traveler. A return trip to a country where you've previously followed the standard sightseeing routes can reveal a completely different world.

Once those glossy catalogs with their vivid photos start arriving in your mailbox, you'll probably be like a child in an ice cream store, vacillating among a wealth of choices. When you find trips that appeal to you, call the companies and ask for detailed itineraries.

After you've narrowed your choices to two or three dream destinations, you need to find answers to some important questions. And you'll have to dig deeper than the trip descriptions provided by the companies. To be sure you take the right trip at the right time, research such factors as weather variables and disease risks. And take a close look at the current situations of each country on your wish list: Is there political unrest or criminal activity? Anything brewing that might bring a little more excitement that you've bargained for?

EXCITEMENT . . . OR DANGER

Adventure travel companies tell you to "expect the unexpected." Even so, you probably don't think that includes highway bandits, urban kidnappers, or outback guerrillas. Adventure travel companies don't go to places where you might encounter excitement like that, do they?

Yes, sometimes they do. But it's important to remember that in such cases it's generally a calculated risk where the odds are very low that anything bad will happen to you. Nevertheless, you need to do your own risk assessment. Take the pulse of the countries you're considering, checking up on any security threats that might mar your trip. Is the government stable? Check the six-month prognosis: You don't want to plan a trip to a country where a simmering insurgency is about to break out into a rolling boil, or one where a neighbor is poised with troops on the border or terrorists in the jungle.

The foreign news sections of national newspapers and magazines are good sources of information. Check the short reports from news services such as Reuters, as well as the longer, in-depth features by foreign correspondents. The Overseas Security Advisory Council has information on threats, incidents, and terrorist groups. Call for a State Department traveler's update fax. These consular information sheets present current information on such topics as crime, terrorist activities, medical facilities, aviation, security concerns, areas of instability, and road safety. (See Appendix, page 159, for contact information.)

As you do your research, patterns might emerge that will indicate possible trouble some months ahead. For instance, when a country's economy takes a nosedive, skyrocketing robberies often follow a currency devaluation, turning once safe places into danger zones. Scattered or sporadic political incidents might be the early warning signs of an emerging area of revolutionary instability. Other circumstances warrant a caution light: a wave of anti-American sentiment or refugee spillover from tribal warfare.

> **TIP**
>
> Read between the lines of State Department advisories. Dangerous incidents might not always be given equal weight. Political considerations might shade the wording: stronger for disfavored countries (such as an official warning against travel), veiled for other countries (even though their incidents might be more alarming).

Most adventure travel destinations are relatively safe, but certain popular countries have been on recent "dangerous places" lists compiled by security experts. For instance, Papua New Guinea, an exciting and primitive adventure travel destination, was recently put in the "high risk" category by a major risk-management and security firm that tracks trends and incidents. Other countries on recent lists have included Kenya, with armed robbers in game parks; Guatemala, with bandits ambushing travelers; India, with bombs in bazaars; and Peru, with armed robbers on trekking routes.

Other adventure travel destinations have been in the news recently, such as the demonstrations and explosions in Burma; the kidnapping of foreigners in Vietnam; and the shooting of Americans in Cambodia.

Sounds bad. But you don't necessarily have to cross such places off your wish list; established, experienced adventure travel companies are often able to run successful trips in countries on the "troubled" or "potential hot spot" lists. For example, some companies operated in Peru when the Shining Path rebel movement was active.

The best adventure travel companies have a widespread intelligence network—solid local sources—and are able to make informed decisions about the safety of a particular itinerary. Moreover, their trips often follow routes that are far from the problem areas. These companies say they often know more than the State Department about the safety of the places where they'll be taking their clients. Of course, this claim encompasses a wide range of operations. The good companies have those excellent sources of information on the ground in such countries, while a company without reliable contacts might not be able to make a realistic assessment of the situation.

Companies face a dilemma when trouble is merely brewing—nothing really threatening but perhaps forewarning something worse. Their customers might already have paid in full, and the company wants the business. But they don't want to risk an incident that could harm their reputation or even end their trips to a popular destination. This makes your *own* research of the area all the more important.

Consider a destination country's transportation systems as well. The infrastructure in a developing country might range from unreliable to downright dangerous. That can make internal travel rather dicey. Companies cope with this problem in various ways—and that's something else to look at when deciding on both your destination and your adventure travel company (more on traveling within a country in Chapter 4).

HEALTH RISKS

Take a good look at any health threats you might encounter. Exotic pathogens inhabit many adventure travel countries. Research the medical situation of your destination, including the specific regions and altitudes where you'll be traveling. Call the Centers for Disease Control and Prevention to receive faxed fact sheets on diseases and preventive measures for specific countries.

Predeparture inoculations and trip-in-progress medications can't keep all the bacteria, viruses, and parasites at bay. For instance, malaria is endemic in many adventure travel regions and there are no guaranteed methods of prevention, only drugs that might—or might not—work.

What diseases are endemic—and sometimes suddenly epidemic—where you might go? What sort of preventive vaccines and medications are available? If the answer to your second question is "not much," you might want to reconsider your choice. It won't be the trip of a lifetime if apprehension overwhelms your enjoyment. Your general health and any special physical considerations are factors in deciding how adventurous you want to be.

But just as you shouldn't necessarily let security threats keep you from traveling to a place you'd love to see, don't let health threats automatically cancel out a country. You simply need to know what you're getting into so you can make an informed decision. (See Chapter 5 for details on what lurks in the heart of the jungle—and what you can do about it.)

GOOD VERSUS BAD GOVERNMENTS

You might also want to consider the ethical dilemma of going to a country where the regime represses or tortures people. If the human rights policies of countries such as Iran, Tibet, Indonesia, or Myanmar (Burma) bother you, should you support them by contributing your tourism dollars? There are points to be made on both sides.

Many human rights advocates believe tourism encourages the oppressors. Shutting off income to force a government to change is the best tactic, they say, citing the successful strategy used against South Africa's apartheid regime, when foreign interests withdrew their presence and investments.

In Myanmar, Nobel peace prize laureate Aung San Suu Kyi has asked foreigners to stay away, saying tourism supports authoritarianism. That government is razing native homes and confiscating family farms to build multistory resorts, according to human rights organizations.

But others say the opposite is true: that bringing in tourists from the outside world decreases isolation, brings hope to the people, and heightens world awareness of a country's problems. East Timor in Indonesia is rated by many human rights activists as one of the most repressed countries on earth, yet the East Timorese say tourism is their only means of communicating with the rest of the world.

WHEN TO GO

AT THE RIGHT TIME OF YEAR YOUR DREAM DESTINATION CAN be a paradise. But at the wrong time—such as monsoon season—it can be hell on earth. Only if you time your trip to coincide with the best weather will it look like those bright and sunny catalog photos that were so enticing. You might also want to plan your trip around your destination's peak seasons for lush plants and flowers, wildlife activity, or cultural festivals.

WEATHER

Research the seasons in the countries you're considering. How wet, how cold, how cloudy can it get? Which months have the best average temperatures, the most hours of sunshine? Many regions have regular dry and rainy seasons, so it makes sense to time your trip for the good months. In other regions the seasons are not as well defined, but some months will still have less rain and fewer clouds.

If you have your heart set on a particular region and you're able to get away any time of year, you can just wait until the perfect month and fly off to your first choice country. But maybe there are only certain months when you can take a vacation, or perhaps you can't bear to wait almost a year until the good weather rolls around again at your favorite destination. If so, you need to choose a substitute.

For instance, if you really want to trek up into Nepal's Annapurna Sanctuary but can only get away from your desk in midwinter and midsummer, you'll have to settle for another destination—and put this fall-or-spring-only Sanctuary trek on hold until you switch jobs.

Quite often, your best option is in the opposite hemisphere: When it's gray and icy at home, it's warm and sunny below the equator—the time to head for Machu Picchu or Patagonia, for instance.

Look carefully at the way adventure travel companies describe the climate for the trips you're thinking about. Try to read between the lines—and then do some independent research.

One trip description says that from December through May the days are warm and sunny and that from June through November it's "a bit cooler and breezy but still warm." That sounds okay— and the company does run trips year-round. But how warm is "still warm" and what about the sunshine? Is it at least partially sunny—or is it actually cloudy or foggy much of those other months?

> **TIP**
>
> For many regions, the best time to go is soon after the rainy season, when the countryside is full of the lush vegetation you saw in those catalog photos.

A description of another year-round trip describes a place "where the last of the Atlantic sea turtles nest." True, but they'll only come crawling up onto the beaches at one time of the year.

Don't skip over phrasing like "potential views" of the mountain you have your heart set on seeing. Is low level haze likely at the time you can go? What about fog and clouds? Winter snows?

For instance, take that Annapurna Sanctuary trip, where trekkers camp at 13,500 feet in a peak-ringed bowl: Some companies offer trips into December, while others cut off travel to that high, snowy realm by the end of November. There are similar red-light, green-light considerations for many other adventure travel destinations. For example:

- **Indonesia:** Some companies run trips only during the relatively dry summer months. Others go virtually year-round, despite the big increase in precipitation during the winter "tropical downpour" season.
- **Morocco:** Despite those sunny photos of golden sands, it can be rainy in the winter.
- **Botswana:** Many companies offer trips virtually year-round, but June to October is the best time. November to February is the wetter season.
- **Belize:** Some companies run trips in November and December while others wait until January. Those that hold off have a good reason: By February the average number of days with rainfall has dropped in half. A company that does run trips in November mentions "afternoon showers" in its trip description. However, according to a native, Belize gets "chilly, cloudy weather every year in November, even December."

One helpful company provides the number of "hours of bright sunshine" for each trip's time slots. This figure doesn't count those dim 25-watt days when it's not raining but not exactly picture perfect either. With this sort of trip description you get an accurate view of the conditions you can expect.

Assess each company's weather descriptions for informative honesty. If you're looking at the same basic itinerary, does one gloss over the potential downside while another portrays a more realistic picture? Later, when you're deciding on a specific company, this will be something to keep in mind.

FLORA, FAUNA, AND FESTIVALS

Like the weather, other aspects of the natural world follow seasonal patterns that could affect the timing of your trip. Birders should check nesting times before choosing a trip to see exotic species. Wildlife and flowers have their seasons as well, so check migration patterns and blooming times too. For instance, the Galapagos Islands have many amazing year-round species, including iguanas and sea lions. But if your heart is set on seeing the giant sea turtles, you'd better time your visit for the October–March window.

If you're an ornithologist who wants to add the rare jabiru stork—the largest flying bird in the New World—to your life list, you should time your trip to Belize for the December-to-March nesting season. Or if you're going there to capture a photograph of those incredible little green frogs with the big red eyes—the ones you've seen in all the catalog photos—check out their tadpole-to-adult schedule. Otherwise, you could arrive and be told, "Oh, those little ruby-eyes haven't hatched yet."

In Kenya and Tanzania, the four-month "long rains" end by July, and that's when the massive migration of a million wildebeests takes place. In Zimbabwe, the animals are easier to observe later in the summer's dry season as they cluster around the remaining water holes.

As for seeing blooms: In South Africa, spring flowers peak in October and November, while in Nepal, the towering rhododendrons bloom in spring.

Some of adventure travel's most indelible moments occur at special festivals. What could be better than a visit that coincides with a country's most exciting and colorful celebrations? For instance, you can wait until India's hot and steamy monsoon season ends and catch the Pushkar Camel Fair in drier, cooler November. Festival times for other adventure travel destinations include Papua New Guinea's Sing Sing pageants in August, Bhutan's Paro Tshechu in March, and Mongolia's midsummer Naadam festivals.

Despite all your careful research, you'll probably find you just can't have it all—festivals, flora, fauna, and clear skies—at the same time. In that case, analyze the trade-offs: In Bhutan, for instance, fall is drier, but spring has beautiful flowers—and that spectacular festival.

EXCEPTIONS TO THE RULE

A major weather anomaly can cause pronounced departures from the norms. At the first sign that something big is brewing, look at shifts in the jet stream, global long-range forecasts, and weather records from similar events. For instance, an El Niño hot spot in the Pacific alters upper air circulation patterns and changes the distribution of moisture around the world. This phenomenon can skew a country's weather patterns dramatically, causing torrential rains and flooding during the dry season, or droughts and even wildfires during the rainy season. Adventure travel destinations such as Indonesia, South Africa, Peru, and Ecuador have had severe dry spells or heavy downpours just when they least expected them.

Periods of heavier-than-normal precipitation can cause problems even if you arrive after the clouds are long gone. For instance, if you're going trekking high in the mountains, you could encounter deep, leftover snowfields at a time when you would normally expect clear trails and slopes covered in wildflowers. And if the opposite occurred and the winter rains never came, you might not find the landscapes you expect; the countryside might not have its customary profuse blooms and lush vegetation.

AND WHEN NOT TO GO

In addition to the bad-weather months there can be other less-than-optimal periods for adventure travel.

If you're headed for a country where there is internal strife or border trouble, check the major "anniversary" dates, such as those of uprisings or massacres.

Demonstrations that commemorate such dates can escalate into riots; or even worse, dissident groups might target tourists. Read up on recent history, watching for accounts of troubles occurring on anniversary dates that fall during your planned visit. Have bombs gone off on those dates in recent years? Have there been massive demonstrations or waves of terrorist incidents?

> **TIP**
>
> An El Niño year could be a good time to visit some places in the off season. For instance, Indonesia normally receives about five times as much rain in December as in July, but not during El Niño periods. There might be only a small window of opportunity, however. Severe droughts have led to massive wildfires in Indonesia and other countries.

THE RIGHT KIND OF TRIP FOR YOU

ADVENTURE TRAVEL OFFERS ALL SORTS OF ALTERNATIVES TO sitting on a tour bus. Since adventure travel is an "active" exploration, you'll have a role to play in your first expedition. The next step after zeroing in on your destination is choosing the way you want to see the country. You might want to see it using your own muscle power—paddling, pedaling, or hiking. Or you might opt for a rugged sort of conveyance—floating on a jungle boat, riding a camel, or bouncing along in a Land Rover.

If the thought of paddling in water deeper than five feet scares you breathless, then kayaking sea waters or rafting wild rivers is not for you. But whenever possible, choose a mode of activity and travel that reveals the best of a country's wildlife and cultures.

If you're an experienced cyclist or a seasoned hiker, you probably know what you're getting into if you opt for bicycling or trekking. If you're not, you should get some practical experience in your prospective trip activity. You might find out you're not happy pedaling or tramping day after day. It's much better (and safer) to find out at home rather than halfway around the world.

THE RATINGS GAME

After you've matched a destination to your desires, you need to match a trip to your ability. The ratings that companies use in their catalog descriptions fall into three general categories:

- **Easy** or **leisurely.** Possibly roughing it, could be a good bit of walking, but no great exertion expected.
- **Moderate.** A big range here; people who are relatively fit might get into trouble on trips at the high end of this category.
- **Strenuous** or **rigorous.** Not a category for wannabes— or those looking for a lose-weight-and-get-in-shape substitute for a two-week stay at a spa. The people in this group will have strength and stamina, and you'll be expected to keep up.

There's a lot of leeway in those rating categories. They often mean different things to different companies—and to their customers. After you've narrowed down your choices to a few trips and received detailed itineraries, analyze the effort required—and ask the companies some specific questions.

If it's a bike trip, ask what sort of grades you'll encounter— how steep, how long, how many, and at what altitude. Will the surfaces be hard (and easy) or soft and rocky (much tougher)? If it's a trek, you'll need to know the same sorts of things: the number of miles each day, the type of trail surface, the total elevation gain each day, and how many hours of hiking each day. (A trail that gains 500 feet per mile is a steady climb—

and tiring if you're not in shape, exhausting if it's at high altitude! A gain of 1,000 feet per mile is quite steep.)

Quiz the company if a trip is rated "moderate." You need to explore in depth their interpretation of that label. For instance, a major adventure travel company rated one of its treks moderate, even though the average day involved a seven-hour hike with a 3,000-foot climb over a high mountain pass. One slightly paunchy, somewhat fit middle-aged man who thought he was in sufficient shape for a moderate trek joined one of those trips. He struggled and strained—beet red, breathing hard, and close to apoplexy—barely able to keep up with his group. He survived—but only after a worrisome ten days as a heart attack candidate. The company later relabeled this trek as strenuous.

ARE YOU UP TO THE CHALLENGE?

Hikers often use trail profiles in guidebooks to see if they can handle all the ups and downs ahead. A profile silhouettes the trail's peaks and valleys against a graph: The mileage is laid out horizontally beneath the silhouettes and the elevation is marked vertically on the left side.

One adventure travel company includes trail profiles in its catalogs so you can see at a glance exactly how difficult each day's hike will be—how steep and how far. When you call a company for a detailed itinerary, ask if they can supply a profile. It's a good way to assess whether you'll be able to keep up with the group day after day.

If you're thinking of a moderate raft trip you probably won't need any training or experience, but you should make sure you know what some terms—such as Class IV rapids—mean. There are books and videos that will give you a pretty accurate picture of what sort of roller-coaster ride you could expect.

On a little nature walk, kindness would be a primary consideration and a guide would slow down so the least-able participants could keep up with the rest of the group. But in a wild, remote area there are other factors that dictate the group's speed. The leader will need to keep up the pace in order to get to food, shelter, and water before dark; there could be weather threats, such as lightning, and the group might need to keep moving along quickly in order to get hikers over a mountain pass or paddlers to a river exit before the afternoon thunderstorm.

HIGH PLACES

Some of the best trips go to some of the highest places, such as the Inca Trail in Peru or the Annapurna Sanctuary in Nepal. The spectacular mountains and the incredible views attract accomplished climbers and neophyte flatlanders alike. And even if you're in the latter category, if you've done your aerobic homework you'll be able to participate in just about any moderate-rated trek.

But "into thin air" isn't a term that only applies to Mount Everest heights. At 10,000 feet you'll be operating on just two-thirds of the oxygen at sea level. As you go higher, there's even less oxygen to power your muscles. If you've never gone this high before, you'll be surprised at how you'll slow down and gasp for air, even if you're in good shape.

Even some people who are in great shape have more than the normal problems above 10,000 feet—and some at about 8,000 feet or so. Altitude sickness can incapacitate a fit thirtysomething while a paunchy fiftysomething is able to keep on trucking onward and upward. Generally, it's most likely to strike those who live below 3,000 feet, are under age 20, are overweight, or are in poor physical condition.

No matter your degree of susceptibility, there are things you should know before you decide on a high altitude trek. There are three types of altitude sickness:

- **Acute mountain sickness,** which typically includes headache, fatigue, loss of appetite, nausea, dizziness, and insomnia. In milder reactions, these symptoms dissipate fairly quickly as the body adjusts to the thinner air.
- **High altitude pulmonary edema (HAPE),** a buildup of fluid in the lungs. Symptoms are persistent cough, shortness of breath, weakness, and pale or even blue color.
- **High altitude cerebral edema (HACE),** a buildup of fluid on the brain that can progress rapidly to coma and death. Symptoms are severe headache, dizziness, confusion, vomiting, and seizures.

HAPE and HACE are extremely serious conditions, and immediate descent is urgent, continuing until the symptoms cease. Some trips—generally those rated strenuous that flirt with the 20,000-foot superlevel—carry oxygen and even a Gamow bag for immediate care in cases of HACE or HAPE.

Unless you have enough experience to know how fast you can ascend, pick a trip that gains altitude relatively slowly. Guidelines vary, but some experts suggest that between 10,000 and 14,000 feet, you should ascend less than 2,000 feet per day; and above 14,000 feet, ascend just 500 feet per day. Another general rule: You should have a rest-and-acclimatization day for every 3,000 feet gained.

ROUGHING IT AND TOUGHING IT: THE LUXURY FACTOR

Risks aside, there's the matter of personal taste when you're choosing a trip. Will you be able to enjoy yourself without the comforts of civilization? Just how down and dirty and rough and tough do you want to get? Trips run the gamut from luxurious to rustic.

> **TIP**
>
> For a mountainous trek, study the detailed itineraries to see which trips allow enough acclimatization time for you. The factor that counts the most is the altitude at which you sleep. You might climb higher during the day, then descend to a campsite. Use the level of the campsites as the benchmark for measuring the rate of ascent.

Usually there's a tradeoff: softer beds vs. stranger sights. Generally, the tougher and longer the distance, the richer the experience. But such trips will demand more of you on every level. In addition to the extra exertion, you might have to put up with sheer discomfort, strange food, and extreme elements.

Few people are up to the challenge of getting the farthest away from it all, so there's less of an economic incentive to build tourist facilities in remote areas. Porters will carry your food, tent, and sleeping bag to such places, but you'll have to leave luxuries—like running water—far behind.

Even if an itinerary specifies a roof over your head, it might be a thatched one. On a trek to Sumatra, for example, your lodgings will be about as far removed from Hilton/Sheraton style as you can get. You'll spend the nights in the homes of tribal villagers—no electricity, no bathroom, no privacy. But you'll be among a handful of the lucky ones who get a chance to participate in the life of such a different culture.

Your personality is another factor to consider. You can't be the sort who expects a written guarantee that everything will go exactly according to plan, or you wouldn't even be thinking about a trip to a primitive part of the world. However, even many third world countries have a beaten path, and trips that follow time-tested routes tend to run more smoothly, with fewer surprises and glitches. A circuit of Costa Rica's national parks and preserves will be quite different from a back-of-beyond tour from Urumchi to Margilan. (Both would be fascinating, but the former perhaps would be better for those who would like to minimize their encounters with extreme and unsettling situations.)

To choose the right trip at the right time, you must research, research, and then research some more. Use your phone and your library; send your mouse out on the Internet for some reconnaissance. Dig for facts like a sleuth. The more you know, the better your choice. And when you've figured out where and when and what sort of trip, it's time to decide who you want to go with—and that will take even more research.

CHAPTER 3

CHOOSING THE RIGHT COMPANY

CHOOSING THE RIGHT ADVENTURE TRAVEL COMPANY IS A crucial step—perhaps more important than choosing your destination or even your traveling companion. Choose well, and you'll be safer, healthier, and happier.

First, make sure any company you're considering limits the number of clients per trip to fifteen. The small group is a hallmark of adventure travel, and reputable companies adhere to this standard. Moving through a country this way, you're much more likely to see rare birds and animals in the wilderness and experience more intimate encounters with the native people in settlements.

Beyond this major criterion, there are a number of factors to consider before making your decision. Look at the following for each company:

- number of years in the business
- type of leaders
- experience, local knowledge, and connections in your destination country
- safety precautions
- trip itineraries
- costs and what you get for your money
- attitude and philosophy
- customer satisfaction

A company with years of experience, a good safety record, solid financial status, local expertise, and an educated attitude is your best bet, especially if the employees are enthusiastic and retain—despite the inevitable corporate structure—a childlike sense of excitement and curiosity. A company that's hungry, with inadequate capital, is more likely to take risks and run trips with flimsy safety nets. And one that's less savvy, with little on-the-ground experience, is more likely to make uninformed decisions.

"This is an unregulated business, full of land mines," says Richard Bangs, founder of one of the oldest adventure travel companies. "You blindly commit a lot of money up front to people you've never met to take you to faraway places where God knows what could happen to you."

When you plunk your money down for a trip to one of those faraway places, to a great extent you will have to commit yourself on trust. But you don't have to go into this blindfolded. Research and interrogation can shine a spotlight on a company's virtues and shortcomings, enabling you to make an educated choice.

EXPERIENCE IS THE BEST TEACHER

IF YOU'RE GOING TO ENTRUST YOURSELF TO A COMPANY THAT will take you to one of those places where anything can happen, an outfit that's "been there, done that" many times for several years is your best choice. One with a record of safe trips and satisfied customers is more likely to bring you back alive—and ready to try more adventures.

An experienced company's trips will run more smoothly. They know the best places to go—and how to get there. The staff members know the best campsites, lodges, routes, and food sources, and they'll choose the most reliable transporta-

tion. They know what to do in case of emergencies, how to duck
trouble, how to evacuate someone quickly and safely, and how
to adapt itineraries on the spot if problems arise.

Ask your prospective adventure travel companies these
questions:

- How many years have you been in business? How many
  years under the same ownership?
- How long have you run the specific trip I'm interested
  in? (A fine company might have run trips for years with
  A+ ratings, yet it could bungle a new trip in the same
  country. Find out if they've run the new trip long enough
  to iron out the wrinkles—you shouldn't pay full price for
  a work in progress.)
- What organizations—museums, nonprofits, corporations,
  universities—have taken trips with you? Which ones are
  repeat customers?
- How much liability insurance do you carry? (Some companies carry $1 million, others $5 million.)
- Are you a member of the U.S. Tour Operators Association? (This organization won't admit companies until
  they've been in business for at least three years. The
  association requires a minimum of $1 million in liability
  insurance; participation in the association's million-dollar
  Consumer Protection Plan, which shelters clients from
  insolvency or bankruptcy losses; references from financial institutions and industry sources; and a certain vol-
  ume of clients and income.)
- Are you a member of the American Society of Travel
  Agents?

TYPES OF LEADERS

The best travel leader has an intimate knowledge and deep
love for his or her assigned country—the language, the culture, the history, and the natural world. This person also has
the maturity to make good decisions in a crisis and the skills
to handle a medical emergency or dangerous situation.

Peruse the various catalogs and you'll see a wide varia-
tion in the descriptions of leaders. Some companies devote
several pages to blurbs about their trip leaders, with color
photos and impressive resumes; others leave little or no space
for this information. But even sketchy bios can be informative: Look for illuminating phrases. One company's catalog

contains such descriptions as "party queen" and "fondness for beer." Others tout such qualifications as "former Peace Corps volunteer," "Ph.D. in marine ecology," or "director of gorilla research station."

Unless you're looking for Greek Week pledge types, you'll be better off in the competent hands of a grown-up. Look for a company whose catalog biographies feature people who:

- have lived in the country for several years
- speak the language fluently
- have a university education
- are interested in wildlife, anthropology, and local culture
- have years of trip-leading experience
- know wilderness, survival, and advanced first-aid skills

While a few outfits will put an inexperienced person in an empty slot, the better companies have trip leaders with years of experience in their assigned country. In addition to their expertise, someone who has lived in a country for a long time is much more likely to respect the people there (and have their respect, as well). As a result, groups traveling with that leader are often welcomed with warmth and treated to genuine hospitality.

There's another clue to look for in leader descriptions. Some people choose adventure travel primarily for the physical challenge of bagging a high peak or running a wild river, while others trek or paddle so they can see primitive regions and remote cultures. If you're the latter type, you'll want to scrutinize trips with companies whose leader descriptions feature such feats as "climbed 200 summits" and "cycled across Siberia"; you might end up as the odd one out in a group of super-athletes.

Finally, ask the company about the guide for the particular trip you're interested in: How long has this person been with the company? How long has this person lived in the country, and how many times has he or she led that

RED FLAG

The good companies are proud of their experienced leaders, and rightly so. If a company's bios don't mention any relevant accomplishments, some of its leaders might be only one step ahead of you in terms of skills and expertise.

IT HAPPENED

The leader on a trek through Moroccan villages was a young woman leading her third trip in that country. She hadn't lived there, didn't know the language, and often violated local customs by failing to cover her bare arms and legs. Her clients were embarrassed and felt her actions reflected badly on all of them in the eyes of the traditional Muslims. Moreover, her actions probably killed their chances for the sort of in-home visits that are highlights of adventure travel.

RED FLAG

You might pick up another clue to the kind of leaders a company has by looking through its old catalogs. With some you'll see many of the same faces year after year, while with others you'll see a complete turnover in a short time. It might be coincidence—but it could be a warning signal.

trip? Is this person able to communicate in all the dialects or languages along the route? And if the guide is a native, does he or she speak fluent English?

LOCAL CONTACTS AND SAFETY PRECAUTIONS

ADVENTURE TRAVEL EXECUTIVES VARY WIDELY IN THEIR knowledge of what's really going on in the far-flung countries they send their clients to. Many visit frequently, cultivate long-standing relationships with skilled guides and outfitters, monitor operations closely, and take actual trips with clients. They know the region, the language, the attitudes, and the politics.

But others operate with a handful of people who run everything by phone from the mainland. They let their fingers do the walking, subcontracting trips to distant outfits without making personal trips to investigate them or check up on them periodically. One company with two staff members runs fifty trips per year, and each staffer goes out in the field for only one trip per year. In essence, this is more of a "wholesale" operation than a "hands-on" operation.

Local savvy and contacts are important not only for safety but for the quality of the logistics and the expertise of the leadership. Quiz the companies you're considering to get a better idea of which ones actually have in-depth experience in your destination country. Ask them:

- How often do you visit the country?
- Do you design and test your own trips?
- Do you use your own staff?
- If not, for how many years have you used your outfitter?
- Have you taken one of your company's trips with this outfitter?
- Do you have offices in some of your destination countries?
- Are you still running trips to regions where there's increased danger—from weather anomalies to terrorist actions—when other companies have stopped running trips to those places?
- How would you handle a medical emergency at the most remote point of the trip?

If the in-office specialist for a particular region can't come up with a solid answer to that last question, it could be a sign that the outfit might rely on a subcontractor to "wing it" if someone gets very sick or badly injured. The complexity of a company's emergency plans is a good indication of its safety emphasis. For instance, one company that runs raft trips on a remote third world river has detailed maps showing exit trails and emergency vehicles. They know where to find helicopters and clean blood supplies. And the guides have medical training and carry wilderness medicine emergency kits.

If a company has contingency plans worked out for each day of the itinerary, it's a sign it has solid on-the-ground contacts and in-depth knowledge of the country's infrastructure—which would come in handy in the event of sudden political unrest.

In today's volatile developing countries, local opposition to the government can mean danger for tourists. A savvy company's local knowledge can steer you away from trouble, while one with poor experience or lack of local contacts can steer you right into it.

A company that keeps its eyes open and ears to the ground at your destination will run a safer trip. The executives or staff will spot questionable practices, hear about problems, and learn about emerging unrest.

Another way to assess the differences between companies is to compare their arrangements for the same basic trip.

For a rugged or remote trip, compare the staff-to-client ratios. A company with a relatively smaller staff might not have enough help to spare in case one or more clients becomes ill or injured. The better outfits can leave a porter with one injured client and spare a second staffer to take another client to a lower level to alleviate altitude sickness.

A company's support system is indicative of its safety attitude. For instance, on a bike trip in Vietnam, one safety-conscious company provides a vehicle that dispenses snacks and safe drinking water, an ambulance, four translators, and four security people. Another company takes a Gamow bag on its high-altitude trips. If someone gets critically ill with

IT HAPPENED

Remember that story about the company whose clients were ambushed and killed? Here are the details. The adventure travelers were crossing a remote region of a troubled third world country in three vehicles. Instead of following the "official" route, one driver took a short-cut—and ended up in rebel territory. His van was stopped by guerillas toting automatic weapons. They ordered everyone out, lined them up on the side of the road, and began shooting. One man fell and started rolling downhill an instant before the hail of bullets reached his part of the line. He was the only one who survived to tell the tale.

IT HAPPENED

A river rafting company in South America sold its equipment to a local group who wanted to take over operations on an Andean river. The new outfitter's first assignment was its last. The inexperienced leaders missed their takeout spot—the last place where it was possible to pull out of the current and into a quiet eddy and disembark on a riverbank. The helpless rafters were swept on as the river began its plunge through miles of froth and foam, rocks and rapids that no humans on rubber rafts could survive.

altitude sickness, this bag can provide fast relief of symptoms by simulating a descent to 5,000 feet.

Ask about the company's brands of camping equipment. Tents and sleeping bags made by one of the better manufacturers will keep you drier and warmer than those purchased from an off-brand surplus dealer. (A good outdoors store can advise you about brands.)

> **RED FLAG**
>
> Think twice about a company that downplays the difficulty of its trips or the need for pretrip physical conditioning. If other companies advise tougher training regimens and rate similar trips as tougher, it's reason to wonder about that easygoing company's safety attitudes.

COMPARING ITINERARIES

IT'S HARD TO FIND A TRIP ITINERARY THAT *DOESN'T* SOUND wonderful—they all look like day after day of the most fascinating times you could ever have. But close scrutiny of itineraries will reveal a lot about a company. You'll spot telltale signs that one company might be more interested in cutting corners than in watching out for your best interests. And you'll see details that indicate another company has gone to great lengths to provide exceptional experiences.

Ask the same questions of each company you're considering and compare their responses: Where do clients spend the nights? How safe (health-wise) are the lodgings? For instance, on basically the same route in Nepal, some trips stop for the night in local teahouses, some stay in lodges built specifically for trekkers, and some camp in tents. Naturally, the cultural experiences will be richer for those sleeping in the native teahouses, but problems with the sanitary conditions have led to illnesses for some of those travelers. In contrast, in company lodges the food and lodging generally meet high sanitary standards. On a recent two-week trip to Nepal's Annapurna region, an entire group of fifteen trekkers staying in those lodges remained healthy—no debilitating episodes of intestinal illness.

At first glance, any itinerary that puts a roof over your head at the end of each day might seem better than one that uses tent sites. But camping might offer the most dramatic dusk and dawn views—wondrous sights just when you have the leisure to sit and absorb that day's finest moments. With tents, one night you might camp near a civilized spot where you could meet the villagers; another night you might enjoy solitary splendor across a valley from a spectacular peak. And of course, you're much more likely to hear exciting sounds, such as the lions' midnight roars or the baboons' predawn howls.

TIP

Speaking of spectacular peaks, here's something to ask about specifically: "Will we get the same view as the photo on page 73 of your catalog? Which day of the trip?" If you're entranced by the gorgeous glossies, make sure you'll be able to eyeball the same scenes.

TIP

For any trek, ask specific questions about the sort of paths you'll follow. You might not be too comfortable if you find yourself on a skinny trail along a cliff with a sheer drop-off.

RED FLAG

Think twice about a company that gets its clients to the top and back in less time than the others. At first glance, it's a more attractive choice—a shorter, cheaper trip to see the same peaks. But this kind of cost-cutting means trekkers are more likely to suffer from acute mountain sickness—or one of the deadly serious versions of altitude edema.

TIP

Wherever you're going, when considering itineraries try to match the length of your trip to your tolerance for group travel. Even ten days traveling as a pack is a little too long for some people.

Note which companies let you spend the night next to the special attractions you'll visit. Late afternoon and early morning are often the best times to see a famous place, when the other tourists have gone and the ambiance comes close to that of the early civilization that built it. For example, ask:

- At Tikal, will I stay at the nearby hotel so I can walk to the ruins, climb a pyramid, and watch the parrots fly to their nighttime nests?
- At Machu Picchu, will you put me on a bus back down the winding mountain road? Or will I stay in the hotel next to the site so I can photograph the ruins sans tourists at sunrise?
- At Marrakesh, will I stay on the outskirts, or will my hotel be within a block or so of the fabled medina and the "Djemaa" square bustling with snake charmers and Arabian Nights scenes?

Compare trips to the same region. Which companies use the standard tourist-trodden routes and which have pioneered new, off-the-beaten-path routes? For instance, one organization offers a Himalayan trip where you "probably will not encounter any other trekkers" along their route, which is "not shown in books . . . not on trekking maps."

Ask about the rate of ascent for the same basic mountain itinerary: On a trip to high altitudes, do you allow hikers sufficient time to acclimatize? In the thinner air, do you gain elevation slowly and allow rest days? If the trip involves significant climbs, compare the number of days in each company's itinerary before the maximum altitude is attained.

ECO-ATTITUDES

EVERYONE WANTS TO MAKE A LIVING, BUT BEYOND THAT there are some travel company executives who are in this business because they love the places they go and the people who live there. And they want to share—and preserve—the wonder of it all.

If you call and ask a lot of questions, not just about the trips but about the region itself, you can probably tell if the outfit is just in it for the money—those usually are the ones with the least sensitivity for the cultures and the environment. *Ecotourism* is a popular buzzword these days, but you should quiz a company to see if that concept is really part of its operating philosophy.

TIP

Devastating deforestation is rampant in much of the developing world. If you're going to a region where the trees are disappearing, ask the company if firewood is used to cook and heat water. The answer will give a clue to the company's "ecosensitivity."

Find out if companies you're considering support ongoing efforts to preserve local cultures and ecosystems. And see if their answers reflect respect for indigenous people and the land their tours traverse.

A company's level of cultural and natural sensitivity is also a good gauge of the types of clients it attracts. If you travel in order to learn and understand, you'll be more comfortable with others who feel the same way—rather than those "ugly American" types who insult and intrude when they encounter local cultures.

YOUR MONEY'S WORTH

YOU CAN USUALLY FIND A LOW-BUDGET TRIP, BUT CHEAPER isn't always better. The travel and staff time necessary to check field operations cost money. So does the logistical support for adventures far afield in rugged regions, especially if some "soft" amenities are included. And of course, the better the ratio of staff to group size, the higher the cost.

Usually the price listed in the trip catalog is the "land cost"—including virtually all your expenses from the time you arrive at the city where you'll meet the group until you're back at the airport for your return flight. But there can be major variations. Some companies include a big-ticket item in their trip costs: your international airfare. And one major company includes medical/evacuation insurance with no dollar limits on the coverage. On the other hand, some companies don't include the costs for the flights within a region that are part of your itinerary.

When comparing different companies' costs for the same basic trip, check out what's included and what will cost you extra, such as:

- international airfare
- internal airfares
- medical/evacuation insurance
- gratuities to porters, escorts, drivers, and local guides
- park permits and museum entrance fees
- extra "local payment" made in cash to the leader at the start or a cash "trip kitty" contribution for food purchases
- meals (usually lunches or dinners) that are not included
- meals in your rendezvous city at the beginning and end of the trip
- airport transfers
- excursions and side trips

Days "at leisure" in the itinerary are great opportunities to explore on your own. But you should be aware that you'll be on your own financially on these days and factor in possible costs.

After you've perused a lot of catalogs, you'll recognize code words indicating things mentioned in the itinerary that aren't included in the cost of the trip. You'll shell out extra bucks if you want to go to the places where you "can see," "can view," or "can visit" the attractions. "Optional" also means you can opt to pay for this on your own.

Adventure travel trips usually begin their "all expenses paid" portion near an international airport—but not always. You might have to pay for your round-trip transportation to the group's meeting place after you reach your destination country.

TIP

In that fine print at the back of the catalogs you'll often see an "exceptional cost increase" clause that gives the company the right to raise the price of any trip at any time prior to departure if there's a major currency fluctuation. This could also work to your advantage, though: If your destination's currency collapses in the interval between the time you sign up and the time you leave, you might be able to negotiate a price reduction. And check with your airline as well—international carriers often reduce their fares to regions that are experiencing economic downturns.

BUDGET OR DELUXE?

There are some times when less *is* more. In addition to leaving more money in your bank account, there are other advantages to lower-cost trips.

Quite often, the less you spend, the fewer the barriers between you and the native people of the places you're visiting. Luxury increases the physical and social distance between you and the local inhabitants, particularly in the eyes of those who live there. Give up some of the creature comforts—the trade-off is well worth it. Staying safe and healthy are the prime considerations and certainly worth paying extra for. But beyond that you don't need all the accouterments of Western civilization. Typically, the fewer the luxuries, the richer your experience is likely to be.

Those who choose less luxurious adventure travel trips tend to be more flexible, relaxed, and adventuresome. They don't worry as much about getting their money's worth, and they don't feel as entitled to attention and perfection. When things don't work out quite right they're much more apt stay calm, even laugh about it. Since you'll be in close quarters with your group for several days, they just might be the best kind of folks to be stuck with.

There is an additional advantage: In cities where there is a potential for terrorist bombings or shootings, you'll be safer in your cheaper, smaller inn. The tourist group in that big, expensive, high-rise hotel will be a much more obvious target.

On the other hand, sometimes there's a good reason to pay more—one that has nothing to do with luxury: The trips that go the farthest off the beaten path usually cost more. If you want to travel routes where you won't see other tourists, or if you want to visit people who haven't seen other foreigners, you'll probably have to pay extra for the added logistics, permits, and expertise required to get you there. Bhutan, for instance, severely limits the number of tourists allowed in each year. A trip to this semiprivate realm might cost twice as much as a trip to Nepal, but about one-third of that higher trip price will go directly to the government for permits. In East Africa you can watch a lion eat its kill "alone" (with your group), or you can share the moment with ten other tour groups—depending on whether your company follows a standard vans-lodges route or one that's more expensive but less traveled.

> **TIP**
>
> If you're looking for erudite companions and Ph.D. lectures, you might consider an adventure travel trip with a museum or university. Costs can sometimes be much higher, however. For instance, an adventure travel company's jungle trip under the auspices of a museum was $800 more than their same basic trip sans the professor.

OTHER COSTS

Once you've determined the bottom line for the cost of the trip you want, you'll probably have some additional expenses:

- **Special equipment.** Going on a bicycling trip that promises hours in the saddle each day? If you don't already have cycling gear, you might want to buy special

TIP

Check with the major foreign airline that flies to your destination—they might pay for your hotel in a big city in their own country. A company that includes your international airfare might also give you a free stopover night.

TIP

Because singles make up a big segment of their market, most adventure travel companies will try to match solo travelers with room- or tent-mates so their clients can avoid paying the "single supplement" fee for private rooms. But if the math doesn't work out and you end up being the odd-numbered "extra" member of the group, you might have to pay hundreds of dollars more for that single supplement. If you don't want to gamble, look for a company that will waive the single supplement if it can't find someone to share accommodations with you.

TIP

Always ask your adventure travel company about special deals. Potential discounts include "early bird" if you book far in advance; "frequent traveler" if you book a second trip; and "add-ons" if you combine two trips.

RED FLAG

Beware of a company that ignores your requests for references or drags its feet for months before coming up with a couple of names. A reputable company with a stable of happy clients will get a list to you very quickly.

shoes, padded shorts, a gel-filled seat, and, if the company doesn't supply one, a helmet (definitely). A paddling trip? You might need neoprene from head to toe to stay warm.

- **Immunizations.** Depending on your destination, the shots you'll need could cost hundreds of dollars. Many health insurance plans don't cover the more exotic travel vaccines.
- **Airfares.** Even if your international flight is included in your trip cost, you'll probably have to pay for your flight to a coastal "gateway" city on the East or West Coast, usually Boston, New York, or Los Angeles.
- **Insurance.** Since you'll be laying out thousands of dollars up front, you'll want trip-interruption and cancellation insurance. And since your own health insurance won't get you helicoptered out of the boondocks or pay on the spot for medical treatment overseas, you'll need an evacuation and emergency medical policy as well.
- **Hotels.** If you go halfway around the world, you might have to spring for a hotel in a stopover city—adding another $200 or so to your costs.

CHECKING REFERENCES

BEFORE YOU SIGN ON THE DOTTED LINE, SEE what others have to say about the company you're interested in. Any outfit worth dealing with will be happy to promptly provide you with a list of previous clients and their phone numbers. Ask for a list of people who have taken the trip you're thinking of.

Adventure travel companies screen their clients to see if they should use their names as references. Naturally, they don't ask anyone who was on a trip with too many mistakes and misadventures. Nevertheless, conversations with these experienced travelers can yield a lot of useful information. You should also ask for contacts and phone numbers at organizations such as universities and professional groups that have been repeat customers.

Call references for each company you're considering and ask:

- How many people were in your group?
- What about the staff-to-client ratio? Was it enough to provide what was needed or was it stretched thin?
- Was your leader fluent in the local language? Was he or she knowledgeable about local flora, fauna, and cultures—and enthusiastic about sharing that knowledge?
- Did your leader know people in the villages? Did he or she provide opportunities for you to visit with people?
- Were all your local guides knowledgeable?
- When did you go? What was the weather like? How was the visibility?
- Did you see lots of other tourists along the way or did your itinerary take you off the beaten path?
- Did your transport vehicles have enough seats and windows so everyone could get a good view of wildlife and landscapes?
- Did your guides know how to find the best game-viewing spots? Did they get you out early enough in the morning? Late enough in the day? Were they able to find and identify wild birds?
- Did people get sick on the trip?
- Did the staff follow sanitary procedures?
- Did the leader take you to clean places to eat, whether a home or a restaurant?
- Did you stay in native abodes? Did they meet minimum standards of cleanliness?
- Were all your vehicles in good condition? Were the drivers careful?
- What about the airline safety on your internal flights?
- Did the staff pack out all the inorganic refuse?

TIP

Experienced adventure travelers are a great resource. When you get these people on the phone, don't limit your questions to the trip you're thinking of taking. Find out if they've taken trips with other companies—and if so, what did they think about the way *those* outfits ran things? Do they have friends who've taken adventure travel trips? Would they give you their names and numbers? If you grill all these experienced travelers, you'll get information you'll never get from the companies. After all, those for-profit entities don't want to reveal details about mistakes made or good trips gone wrong.

RED FLAG

Remember those climate stats. Think twice about a company that offers trips to a region in more months than any of the others. It might care more about its profits than its clients. You might find that the weather is marginal—or downright rainy—in those extra months. If you're thinking about signing up for a trip during a questionable weather month, ask for the names of people who took the trip at that time of year.

- Did the staff treat the local people and the land with respect?
- Were they careful not to disturb fragile areas? Nesting sites? Animals with young?
- Was the trip rated accurately?
- Was the trip what you expected? Did it live up to its advance billing?
- Did the participants' abilities match the designated level—or did the company fill the last slots with people who should have taken an easier trip?
- Were there any emergencies? How well did the leader handle them?
- Did the company send extensive and informative pretrip materials well ahead of time?

TIP

Newspaper travel sections sometimes run articles on local travel agents, noting their specialties. Check with your local travel editor to see if there's such a feature in a back issue. You'll probably spot at least a couple of agencies who say they're adventure travel specialists.

TIP

When you call to find out who else is in your group, ask about their ages. There's a wide range in the typical adventure travel group, but that might not be true if a large group of friends happened to sign up for the trip you want. You could end up being the only one two decades older or younger than everyone else—which might or might not be all right. Catalog photos will yield a few clues as well. If most of the shots show travelers with a few gray hairs and a few facial lines, you'll know that these probably are trips for aging baby boomers and beyond. And if another company's catalog is full of fresh-faced youngsters, you can expect similar companions on most of that company's trips.

RED FLAG

Don't be too impressed just because an agency bills itself as an adventure travel specialist. "Special interest travel certificates" on their walls might only mean they took a two-day course that included an adventure travel component along with a heavy dose of marketing strategies.

MORE TIPS AND TIDBITS

When you've narrowed your choice to a specific trip with a specific company, find out who's already signed up and where they're from. If everyone else is from the same town or the same organization, you might be the odd one out in conversation. Or if you're one of a few individuals added to an organization's trip at the last minute, you might get second-best treatment.

You could find yourself the odd one out in another way as well: Even with a big U.S. company you could find yourself in a group where all the other clients are from another country, which could affect the quality of your trip in an unexpected way. For example, one non–Spanish-speaking American traveler signed up as a single for a trip to Peru. Everyone else in her group was Mexican. Even though others in the group were polite and bilingual, they quite naturally spoke Spanish much of the time. Worse than that, the bilingual trip leader began his explanations and directions in English but soon switched to Spanish as well.

Ask the company if the leader or a company representative will be available until the group leaves the country. Once you're back at your hotel on the last day, with your transportation to the air-port all arranged, you might think, "I don't need that kind of baby-sitting." But you could encounter a problem that only someone familiar with that country could solve.

CAN A TRAVEL AGENT HELP?

IT CAN BE HARD TO FIND A TRAVEL AGENT WHO WILL CALL the adventure travel companies and ask enough questions— or even some of the *right* questions. For many years, agents usually were much more familiar with standard tours, resorts, and cruises; most didn't have a clue about adventure travel trips or companies beyond recognizing a couple of the big names. But the market for adventure travel is growing rapidly, and so more and more travel agencies are beginning to specialize in this area.

Call a few agencies and ask questions to see if they know at least as much as you do after reading all the catalogs. Ask how many clients they've sent adventure traveling in the last year, where, and with whom.

Ask your agent how many companies he or she works with. Agents often latch on to a cou-ple of companies that have worked out with no complaints from their clients—but that kind of background doesn't produce the best trip for you. It's better to do the research yourself until you find an agent who knows adventure travel as well as many know cruise ships and luxury destinations.

With luck, you'll find an agent who is knowledgeable about adventure travel. But even if you have to do all your own legwork, it's still better to get a travel agent involved once you know where and when—and with whom— you want to travel. The agent can make some preliminary inquires to help you get the times and flights you need and find the lowest air-fares. Moreover, when you're ready to make final arrangements, it's best to have an agent make them for you. That way you'll have a backup if there's a glitch later on, such as lost vouchers or canceled flights.

IT HAPPENED

The adventure travel company's trip included airfare from the U.S. It had filled up most of the slots with members of a bird-watching club and had five seats left on the flight, which were sold to individuals. Once the plane landed, segregation ensued: The club members and the five add-ons were separated, with the bird club folks getting more expertise, better accommodations, and more modern transportation.

IT HAPPENED

After a week in the Galapagos, the adventure travelers arrived at the air-port to find the check-in desk mobbed. By coincidence, it was the end of the Easter holiday, and crowds of vacation-ing Ecuadorians all wanted to return home to the mainland. There were no lines—just a chaotic crowd surging forward. Reservations meant nothing. There was just one flight leaving per day, and those who managed to push their way onto the tarmac got on the plane. The rest were stranded. The same thing happened again the next day. One adventure traveler was stranded for three more days before she finally got on a plane.

You can also expect an agent to check on the company's bottom line. According to the American Society of Travel Agents, it's the agent's responsibility to make sure any adventure travel company you choose is financially stable, to ensure that it won't go under before—or during—your trip, that it will pay its in-country expenses so your guide won't desert you midtrip because he or she hasn't been paid, and that it operates safely and carries liability insurance.

CHAPTER 4

CARRIERS AND CONTRACTS

B Y NOW YOU PROBABLY THINK YOU'VE DONE ENOUGH digging to qualify for a private investigator's license. But before you plunk your money down, there are a few more things you should check on, including the kind of transportation your prospective adventure travel company will provide.

Flying to a third world destination is trickier—and sometimes riskier—than flying to New York. Now's the time to find an affordable *but safe* flight. If your international flight is included in your company's package, check on the airline they've chosen. And if your itinerary includes internal flights in your destination country, check out your company's judgment with respect to those carriers as well.

FLIGHT SAFETY

Most domestic travelers know that the most danger-ous part of their trip is the drive to the airport, not the flight. U.S. air carriers have intensive pilot training, strict mainte-nance standards, and outstanding safety records.

Some foreign airlines have none of the above. And many fall between the two extremes. A few adventure travel compa-nies include the international flight as part of the price, which means you might fly from your coastal "gateway" city on an air-line with an unfamiliar name, such as Garuda, Saeta, Lasca, or Taca. Such airlines might not have the stature or records of major international airlines, but at least they've passed one test: They're allowed to take off and land at U.S. airports.

Other airlines are banned from the United States. Recent lists of airlines banned by the Federal Aviation Administration (FAA) have included carriers from Belize, Uruguay, and Zim-babwe. The airlines of Turkey and Guatemala have been on "conditional" lists.

If your international flight is included in the price of the trip you want, and if that flight is on an airline you've never heard of, do some checking around:

- Ask the FAA if the airline has recently been blacklisted from U.S. landings.
- Ask the International Airline Passengers Association about the airline's fleet and safety record.
- Ask travel planners at major corporations if the airline is on their forbidden list (ask friends at large companies to check for you if necessary).
- Ask your travel agent what he or she knows about the air-line.

If something about the airline makes you nervous, ask your adventure travel company if you can get a "land only" price that doesn't include the airfare. Then, if you prefer, you can arrange your own flight with an airline of your choice, one whose record you're comfortable with. If you're unable to find a major U.S. or international airline for your trip, you might find an airline that's affiliated with one of these carriers. For-eign airlines with these connections are more likely to adhere to good maintenance standards—and you're also more likely to collect frequent flier miles.

With the majority of adventure travel companies, however,

you purchase a "land only" package and arrange your own international flight with the airline of your choosing. Most adventure travel companies will be happy to reserve a flight for you, but you should compare the price they offer with that of your travel agent—and with what you can scope out on your own.

When you're comparison shopping for fares, you might want to see what a consolidator can offer. If you use one, book with your credit card through your travel agent—and make sure the consolidator your travel agent recommends is one he or she has been dealing with successfully for some time. These "bucket shops" often have good deals on international flights—but be careful. Sometimes when travelers purchase tickets from consolidators, they are told they're confirmed but arrive at the airport to find out they're on a waiting list.

Don't take a chance on missing your trip's departure just to save money. On an adventure travel trip, a waiting list could be a disaster. You must get to the starting point on time. It's like going on a cruise—they'll pull out right on schedule, with or without you. And some of the overseas rendezvous where groups assemble aren't easy to get to. Flights don't land there four times a day. In fact, sometimes flights don't even land four times a week!

When you're deciding on an airline, the current state of international tensions might be another factor. During times of critical risks of terrorism, you might want to consider flying with a "neutral" national airline such as SAS or SwissAir rather than on a U.S. flagship.

> **RED FLAG**
>
> The airlines in a country whose economy is on a downward spiral could be in the same trouble as the country's other industries. There might be a correlation between the plunging currency and the airlines' finances—less money for maintenance, more hours for pilots, and less of a safety margin.
>
> **TIP**
>
> If you arrange your own international air travel for a trip that normally includes such flights, there are a couple of disadvantages: You'll probably have to pay more, maybe a lot more; and instead of being met at the airport, you'll probably have to make your way to your initial hotel on your own at your own cost.
>
> **TIP**
>
> Some countries' national airlines offer free stopovers, complete with hotel, buffet breakfast, and round-trip transportation to and from the airport. This can be a great way to see a foreign city you never would otherwise. It's a travel bargain to look for when researching your flight plans.
>
> **TIP**
>
> If you get your overseas ticket through a consolidator, you might not be able to collect or use frequent flier miles.

GETTING AROUND ON THE GROUND

AFTER YOU'VE GOTTEN SAFELY ON THE GROUND IN YOUR destination country, you might have more flights ahead of you on that country's domestic airlines. And in some countries, a "national airline" might not match your concept of that phrase!

If your itinerary includes what adventure travel companies call "internal flights," do some more checking. Once again, you want to make sure that any risks you take will be based on an informed decision. (See the "Safety and Security Information" section of the Appendix, page 159, for contact information.)

One way to judge the safety of a country's domestic airlines is to check blacklists. The Department of Defense prohibits travel by its personnel on certain carriers in countries that are not exercising adequate safety oversight. Corporations keep similar lists. Recent lists have included airlines in such adventure travel spots as Belize, Guatemala, Indonesia, Peru, and Zimbabwe.

One airline safety organization has cautioned travelers about certain foreign airlines. For instance, in the past they've warned travelers about India's domestic flights, citing sobering statistics for fatal accidents. Nor was the group bullish on China, which had licensed dozens of questionable new airlines and permitted some pilots to average an alarming seventy hours per week. This group also worried about this country's aircraft maintenance and the many airports without radar or instrument flight equipment.

Some adventure travel companies charter flights for their clients. For instance, one organization uses a private Boeing 757 in Asia. This can be a good alternative, but in a developing country there can sometimes be problems even with this approach. Of course, sometimes flights like these are the only way to get to where you want to go. And even though mishaps are somewhat more likely in undeveloped regions, the odds are still very much in your favor. Thousands go every year to remote spots around the globe and return safe and sound.

Sometimes adventure travelers are faced with problems with *all* their transportation options. For instance, in Guatemala recently, air carriers were on the Defense Department's banned list while at the same time the State Department was saying that travel by road, particularly in tourist vans, was difficult and dangerous.

Travelers with their hearts set on visiting Cambodia's Angkor Wat recently faced a similar dilemma. The companies running trips to this temple complex were flying to Phnom Penh's airport, which no longer met the International Civil Aviation Organization's operational standards. And after that, surface transportation to Angkor Wat posed further risks: Boat travel was dangerous, according to the State Department, but so was travel by train or motor vehicle.

COUNTRY ROADS

Wherever you go, chances are you'll be traveling some country road in the back of beyond. The scenery will be more dramatic—and in most cases the road hazards will be more dramatic as well. This is one more reason to make the effort to choose the most reliable company for your particular trip.

The capital cities in many developing countries look quite modern and familiar— paved roads, neon lights, skyscrapers, even some signs in English. But the exurbs seem like another country entirely. The roads will be primitive: rocks, ruts, blind curves, mountain switchbacks with no guardrails. And many of the drivers—piloting anything from jalopies to 18-wheelers—have primitive driving skills. Even if they have licenses, they might not necessarily be "trained." As for the vehicles, maintenance and safety inspections might be alien concepts.

The State Department's consular information sheets describe road conditions in developing countries. Certain warnings crop up again and again, and quite often they're for adventure travel destinations:

- Highways are poorly maintained and always congested.
- Large animals on roads cause frequent fatal accidents.
- Drivers on inland and rural roads are less likely to comply with basic traffic safety procedures.
- Vehicles pass on narrow mountain roads or on foggy coastal highways.
- Expect excessive speed, unpredictable driving habits, and a lack of basic safety equipment on many vehicles.
- Vehicles sometimes travel with few or no lights.
- Driving at night is particularly hazardous and strongly discouraged.

TIP

Some travel insurance companies won't cover you if you fly on one of their banned airlines. After you've chosen a trip and an adventure travel company—but before you sign up and pay your deposit—don't forget to run all the carriers by the insurance company you intend to use (see "Insuring Your Investment," page 50).

IT HAPPENED

A museum arranged an African safari and chartered a plane to take its adventure travelers to a game area. But the plane ran out of gas and had to make an emergency landing in the middle of nowhere out on the veldt. All ended well, but it was something of a "fright flight" for those passengers.

TIP

If you'll be traveling by train, know what you're getting into. In some countries there have been reports of passengers being drugged and robbed, sometimes with the use of aerosols sprayed in their compartments while they're asleep on overnight trains. (Some travel product companies sell devices to keep your sliding door shut while you sleep.)

It's especially important to choose an adventure travel company that uses safe vehicles and experienced drivers and schedules its drives for daylight hours in dangerous areas.

Travelers who want more information on road conditions can contact the Association for Safe International Road Travel. This group was founded by a mother after her son was killed in Turkey when the bus he was riding plunged into a ravine—after the passengers had pleaded with the driver to slow down.

CANCELLATIONS

AFTER YOU'VE NARROWED YOUR CHOICE TO ONE COMPANY, you'll want to make sure they'll show up at the altar on the big day.

Have you ever been left standing at the gate when your airline canceled your flight "for mechanical reasons"? Did you and your handful of fellow passengers look at each other and think, "Oh sure . . . the real reason they canceled it was because the plane was almost empty." Adventure travel companies cancel for the same reason: Not enough people signed up.

Find out the company's cancellation policy (not just what happens if *you* cancel, but what happens if *they* do). Often a company will reserve the right to cancel a trip if not enough participants sign up. And if this happens, just as often it's not liable for any expenses you might have already incurred. (So if you lose a fortune on your airline tickets, it's your problem.)

The company's right to cancel doesn't have to be part and parcel of your agreement, however. Some companies have certain trips with "guaranteed departures."

> **TIP**
>
> If you book an extension to your trip, write into your contract that any payments made for this add-on excursion will be fully refunded if the company cancels the primary trip.

> **TIP**
>
> Pay for your trip with a credit card if you can. Some companies have a cash-only policy, but avoid paying by check if at all possible. Your credit card company can't make you pay for services you haven't received.

But if your trip isn't in that guaranteed category, how far in advance of the departure date will the company make the decision? Will it run the trip with a certain minimum number of participants? How many are signed up so far? Is there a price differential if the number that actually goes is below a certain minimum?

THE FINE PRINT

NOW YOU'RE ALMOST READY TO SIGN ON THE DOTTED LINE. Ask yourself: Have I done everything I should to make sure I've chosen the right company? In case your research has been a little sloppy, here's an exercise that will focus your mind and intensify your efforts to complete your "homework."

Turn to the very back of the catalog, past the last of the alluring photo spreads. You'll find one or two pages of fine print. Get out your magnifying glass and read this contract, especially the sections with titles like "Terms and Conditions" and "Release of Liability and Assumption of All Risks."

Generally, adventure travel company contracts cover all bets in terms of absolving them from responsibility for losses, damages, injuries, and events such as detention, delays, acts of God, thefts, riots, terrorism, annoyance, quarantine . . . down to "the hotel lost our reservations." And just in case, they also throw in "force majeure"—a handy term to cover whatever might happen that they didn't anticipate or control.

And they cut the strings as far as all the local people and firms they hire. The contract might contain a specific disclaimer, such as one that accepts "no responsibility for the quality or conditions" of the vehicles the company will use. But there will be some sort of general disclaimer as well, that the company is only acting "as agent" for its "contractors" who supply services and transportation, and thus they're "not liable" for what these local people do—or fail to do. That includes everything from "failure to deliver services" to "negligent acts."

To reserve your trip, you'll need to sign this contract, in which basically you acknowledge that you're going on this trip even though you know it's risky and dangerous, you realize that safety standards won't be what you're used to, you understand that you won't have 911 and ER services, and you won't blame the company if you get sick or hurt. The release will conclude with this sort of wording: "I, Alice Adventurer, release Extraordinary Expeditions, Inc. from all liability even though I might get injured, ill, or even die," (signed).

These absolutions are unavoidable, even if you do think the company should be at least partially responsible for your safety and well-being. Ultimately, the company might not be exempt from liability in cases of gross negligence, but nevertheless, this legalese drives home the importance of finding a reputable company.

> **TIP**
>
> Contracts usually have these points that you should keep in mind: (1) If you decide to cancel, notice must be received in writing; and (2) the company has the right to change the trip dates, itinerary, and costs at any time.

INSURING YOUR INVESTMENT

AN ADVENTURE TRAVEL COMPANY PROBABLY WILL REQUIRE you to pay in full two months before your trip date. If you cancel your trip forty-five or thirty days before your departure, you'll get a refund of 25 to 50 percent. But if you have to back out after that, you'll lose it all. Airfare might be the only refundable portion, and even that will depend on the penalties involved.

Those thousands of nonrefundable dollars are a considerable investment. But during that last month or so you could get sick or hurt—so badly that you couldn't travel. What if a routine trip to the doctor turned up a hidden problem requiring immediate surgery? What if you tore a ligament during your weekly tennis game? Can you imagine tramping a Himalayan trail with a cast on your leg? What if something happened to your traveling companion, one of your children, or one of your parents, and you had to stay home to care for him or her?

What if you fell ill halfway through your trip and needed immediate skilled medical care and evacuation back home? Or what if something happened to a family member and you had to cut the trip short? No company will give you a refund for the unused portion.

There is a way to protect your investment even if the worst happens: travel insurance. Your next step is to find the best policy and the best trip insurance company. There are two major categories of travel insurance: (1) trip cancellation/interruption insurance and (2) medical and evacuation insurance.

TRIP CANCELLATION/INTERRUPTION INSURANCE

Trip cancellation/interruption insurance reimburses you for money you will forfeit if you have to cancel a trip or return home in the middle of one. Companies differ in what they offer, but look for clauses that will reimburse you if you miss your trip because of:

- an injury or illness to you, your traveling companion, or a family member that prevents you from traveling
- a court order or jury duty
- an emergency call to duty (other than war)
- a burglary or loss of your home to fire or flood
- a layoff or termination of employment affecting either you or your traveling companion

- a terrorist incident at your destination city within ten days of your arrival date
- an official travel warning issued after you've paid for your trip
- an accident on the way to the airport
- a hijacking

Reimbursement should also be available in case of problems with your adventure travel company, such as:

- strikes or natural disasters that force a cessation of services
- financial default by your adventure travel company or your airline
- nonrefundable payments if your trip is canceled by the adventure travel company

Other coverages to look for include:

- payment of additional accommodation and travel expenses to reach your destination—or rejoin the group—if you are delayed because your traveling companion is hospitalized
- payment of your single supplement charges if your traveling companion cancels or leaves midtrip
- payment of accommodation and travel expenses incurred because of delays of at least twelve hours caused by a traffic accident on the way to the airport; carrier problems, both bad-weather and mechanical; lost or stolen passports, travel documents, or money; strikes; natural disasters; and civil disorder

Baggage insurance is usually available as part of these policies. It covers luggage lost by commercial carriers but not bags that "mysteriously disappear" or are "confiscated" by a foreign government. In general it covers loss of clothing but not other items such as cameras and money. It also might pay for the replacement of essential items if you're delayed by transportation problems for twenty-four hours or more.

For a trip that costs $3,500 including airfare, you can purchase basic trip cancellation/interruption insurance for approximately $200. Extra coverage, such as baggage loss and travel delay, is usually sold as part of a more expensive comprehensive package that includes the medical component.

MEDICAL AND EVACUATION INSURANCE

Medical and evacuation coverage pays for your treatment and evacuation if you become sick or injured while on your trip. It's necessary for several reasons. Your regular medical insurance might not be valid abroad. But even if it is, foreign doctors, clinics, and hospitals often demand immediate cash payment and do not accept checks or credit cards. In addition, for a serious medical emergency, you'll want to get yourself back in the hands of U.S. medical specialists as quickly as possible—and that could cost a fortune. According to the State Department, medical evacuation back to the United States from a remote region of Chile could cost as much as $90,000.

These policies cover problems that are "acute or life-threatening"—not ones that can wait until you get home. The policies generally cover fees for ambulances, physicians, hospital services, surgery, prescribed drugs and supplies, and emergency dental treatment. Transportation covered includes helicopter evacuation, ground carriers, flight to the nearest "adequate" medical facility, airfare back home, and funds for a medical escort recommended by a doctor.

When you're sick or injured in a developing country, the nearest "adequate" care might be several countries away. For instance, when one traveler was hurt in Azerbaijan, his travel insurance company flew him to Finland for emergency treatment.

> **TIP**
>
> If you're over 65, you still need medical insurance. Medicare doesn't cover overseas medical costs.

Premiums vary according to the length of the trip and the maximum amounts allowed for medical treatment and emergency evacuation. For instance, for a two-week trip, a policy with a $10,000 treatment limit and a $50,000 evacuation limit would cost about $70. If this were that $3,500 trip mentioned above, the comprehensive package—coverage for cancellation, interruption, trip delay expenses, baggage, medical treatment, and evacuation—would cost about $290.

COMPARING MORE FINE PRINT

Most insurance companies offer both types of insurance and the combination comprehensive policy.

Finding the right insurance company and policy is a complicated business. Ask your travel agent and adventure travel company for recommendations and check ads in travel magazines. Call a number of travel insurance companies to request their brochures. (See the "Trip and Medical Insurance" section of the Appendix, page 159.)

Carefully compare policies and benefits, evaluating each one's pros and cons. Analyze what you'll get for your money in terms of coverage—and whether each policy will cover what you'll be doing and where you'll be going.

Do your homework thoroughly. Don't automatically accept the policy recommended by your travel agent; it might not cover all the contingencies you're facing.

When you find a policy that seems best for you, get answers to some key questions before signing up:

- When does coverage start? Some companies do not begin coverage until they receive your application at their home office. That leaves you vulnerable for two to six days or more. If your trip is less than two months off, which means you've probably already paid for it, you could lose your entire trip payment if you have bad luck in that two-to-six-day period—you trip and fall and break your arm, or your mother breaks her hip.

- Does the company have a twenty-four-hour hotline? If you have a problem at 3:00 in the morning on a weekend, will you reach a human or an answering machine? This is particularly important if treatment or transportation must be authorized in advance by the company.

- Does the company have a twenty-four-hour emergency translation service? This will be vital if for some reason your trip leader isn't available to act as a go-between.

- In the case of political violence, will the company be able to help with advice and evacuation arrangements?

- How broadly is "family member" defined? Some policies include business partners, grandparents-in-law, step-siblings, nieces and nephews, wards, and legal guardians.

- Will coverage include flights with all the airlines you'll be using—not only your U.S. and international flights but any domestic hops within foreign countries?

- Is travel covered in all the countries you'll be in? For instance, one company's policy might not cover you in Bhutan or Cambodia. Others might require an additional premium if you're going to a place where there's civil unrest. Some companies will not cover travel to any country for which a U.S. government agency has issued an "advisory" or to any country "determined to be unsafe."

- If the State Department issues a travel warning for the country you're going to, will that automatically cancel your insurance?
- Does coverage extend beyond the policy's ending date if you're delayed for a reason that's covered by the policy?
- Does the policy cover bankruptcy by both the airline and the adventure travel company? What about "default" or "failure" to provide services?
- How is "pre-existing condition" defined? Generally, an illness that surfaces during the sixty days before your policy goes into effect is not covered. This might be true even if you haven't been to a doctor and gotten an official diagnosis. If you've had symptoms that in insurance company terms "would cause a prudent person to seek diagnosis or treatment," and you get worse and can't travel, you won't receive benefits. However, some companies will insure you if your condition is controlled—no symptoms or no change in medication. Speaking of which, pay attention to those "medication" clauses. One company won't cover any condition for which medication has been prescribed in the 180 days before your insurance takes effect.
- Is there a limit on coverage for medical evacuation? With some companies, it's $25,000. For a chopper and charter in case of a serious injury or illness, you might have to pay double that amount or more.
- Are all your adventure travel activities covered? If you're going to be using ropes and ice axes to cross a glacier, you might not be covered while you're on the ice. The same goes for scuba diving and Class V rafting.
- Is travel in off-road vehicles covered? Chances are you'll be bouncing along in a four-wheel-drive of some sort at least once during your travels.
- Will the company pay to fly a family member to your bedside if you're hospitalized overseas for more than a week?
- Are dental fees covered—including injury, infection, and loss of filling or tooth?

CHARTING A DECISION

With all the differences in clauses, phrasing, and costs, comparing insurance companies can be difficult. When you've narrowed the field to a few finalists it might help to make a chart.

Across the top list insurance plan features, such as costs, evacuation limits, pre-existing-condition exclusions, etc. Down the left side list the various companies. Go over each plan carefully and note the provisions in each column.

A FEW MORE THINGS TO THINK ABOUT

- Don't just add up all your costs and automatically buy insurance for that amount. You don't need insurance for payments you can ultimately recover, such as refundable airline tickets.
- Look at your contract's "What Is Not Covered" paragraph. Acts of war and civil disorder are often on that list— something to consider if you're going to a region where trouble has already erupted sporadically.
- A few insurance companies have branch offices in adventure travel countries, such as China and Vietnam. A local presence could be a big help in an emergency.
- Ask a company for references, from individual travelers and from organizations— such as museums and corporations—that have used them for a long period of time.
- Take note of everything, even the trip delay time limit. If you miss your connection because you didn't allow "at least three hours" between your connecting flights, you might not be covered. That might not be a reason to go with another company, but it is something to be aware of when booking your flights.
- If you're 75 or older, you might get discouraged by the brochures that specify that coverage is limited to those "age 74 and under." Don't give up, however, because there are some companies that issue policies up to age 85, although they might only offer reduced coverage. (See Appendix, page 159, for help in finding travel insurance companies.)

TIP

Think twice before buying insurance from your adventure travel company. Bankruptcies happen—and if your company goes under not only will your trip be canceled, but the chances are slim that the company will pay any insurance obligations.

FOR WOMEN ONLY

Conditions resulting from pregnancy are often excluded from insurance coverage. Early problems that might require immediate emergency treatment, such as miscarriage or ectopic pregnancy, might not be covered.

TIP

One company starts your insurance coverage at midnight on the day you call to charge your premium. If you wait until the end of the business day to charge your adventure travel trip, you'll be vulnerable for just hours instead of days.

TIP

Some companies will insure you despite any pre-existing conditions—provided you enroll within seven days of making your initial trip deposit.

- If you're taking your children—or grandchildren—look for a company that offers family protection. Some will give children 16 and under full coverage at no additional charge.

PACKAGE DEALS

Occasionally, medical/evacuation insurance is included in the trip's cost if it's part of a package offered by an institution, such as a museum. One major U.S. company routinely provides this insurance for everyone on its trips—without any dollar limits. Which was a good thing in the case of one of their clients, who became extremely ill in Lhasa and was taken to what the adventure travel company calls a "valiant, plucky, and mostly useless" hospital there. The company then arranged and paid for a medically equipped jet complete with doctor and nurse, a flight to a Singapore hospital, and, after one week, first class seats for the patient and an attendant to his home in San Francisco.

If you get hurt or sick on your trip, you'll probably need medical care—even hospitalization—once you get home. Check with your own medical insurance company to make sure your regular coverage dovetails with your plans.

FINAL ARRANGEMENTS

ONCE YOU'VE DONE ALL YOUR RESEARCH AND MADE ALL your decisions, it's finally sign-up time!

Visit your travel agent and finalize your arrangements. You need to get everything signed in concrete at this visit. A lack of coordination in the scheduling could lead to costly mishaps, so have your agent make all your reservations at the same time for: (1) your adventure travel trip; (2) your international flight; and (3) your flight to your gateway city. And if you need to make your own stopover arrangements en route, ask the agent to reserve a hotel for you in that city.

Make sure your agent allows more than adequate time for all your connections. Some travel agents tend to cut it too close, so impress upon yours the crucial importance of catching all your flights so you'll arrive in time to take off on your adventure with your group.

Ask your agent to get your seat assignments at this time if possible or as soon as the airline opens those flights for seat reservations. Some of your flights will be long ones—not the kind where you want to be stuck in a middle seat. If you're next to a window you can nap better; if you're next to an aisle you can get up and get a little exercise more easily.

On the same day you finalize your trip arrangements, purchase your travel and medical insurance by phone, using your credit card, and preferably with a company that will begin your trip cancellation insurance as of midnight that very day. Then all you have to do is play it safe—no climbing ladders or skiing moguls for a few hours—and you'll be home free.

CHAPTER 5

STAYING HEALTHY

ONCE YOU'VE INSURED YOUR PRETRIP HEALTH, IT'S TIME
to concentrate on doing everything you can in advance to
ward off the threats of diseases you might encounter.

Trip catalog descriptions accentuate the positive—without
mentioning the exotic pathogens that populate those exotic destinations. But whether you visit the low jungles or the high
Himalayas, you'll be exposed to health risks unlike anything you
face at home. These include commonly known diseases such as
malaria and cholera, plus a host of strange polysyllabic threats—
like leishmaniasis and schistosomiasis—and some with such
appropriately alarming names as river blindness, sleeping sickness, and hemorrhagic fever. Then there are waterborne parasites,
rodentborne viruses, and insectborne bacteria.

Modern medicine's inoculations can prevent a number of
scourges, but not all. Among the exceptions are some diseases that

are easy to contract and difficult to treat. Some might make you very uncomfortable; a few can kill you.

That's the bad news. The good news is that the vast majority of people go adventure traveling without getting sick. Your destination won't be a "hot zone" teeming with fatal microorganisms such as ebola and lassa fever. And you can take protective measures with vaccinations, insect repellents, and a generous dose of caution.

FOREWARNED IS FOREARMED

TO RESEARCH THE HEALTH RISKS OF YOUR DESTINATION, contact the Centers for Disease Control and Prevention for the relevant country and regional health advisories. You can have these faxed to you, along with the CDC's information sheets on specific diseases, treatments, and vaccines. (For contact information, see the Appendix, page 159.)

The International Association for Medical Assistance to Travellers (IAMAT) can provide a wealth of detailed information, including:

- A world immunization chart with advice on immunizations and preventive measures for 200 countries.
- World charts for malaria, schistosomiasis, and Chagas' disease that detail risk areas and preventive measures. (The malaria chart provides region-specific information on drugs, including brand names, generic names, dosages, frequencies, and manufacturers.)
- World climate charts with not only weather conditions and clothing suggestions but also sanitary conditions. For a number of cities and regions they rate the milk, water, and food, including meats.

IAMAT's world directory lists the English-speaking, Western-trained doctors and their telephone numbers in 125 countries and territories. If you get sick or injured, your trip leader should be able to arrange for competent help. But the leader and group generally move on with their itinerary, and if they must leave you behind you'll feel a lot better if you can communicate with a doctor in your own language. (For contact information at the IAMAT, see the Appendix, page 159.)

Adventure travel companies that run trips to the regions you're interested in also should be able to provide information on everything from inoculations to clothing you'll need to stay

IT HAPPENED

After a severe ankle injury, a traveler ended up in a hospital—in good hands, finally, she thought, after making her way from a remote island to a western European capital. But the doctor spoke only a few words of English—"surgery" and "hospital five weeks." She was left on a gurney in a room with two non–English-speaking nurses who were sterilizing instruments and brandishing syringes. Determined to fly back to U.S. doctors, the patient was barely able to stave off anesthesia by shouting *verboten!* and pointing to her leg.

healthy. Ask them to send you their pre-departure materials for the countries you're considering.

GET THEE TO A TRAVEL CLINIC

Your family doctor might not be the best source for travel medicine advice or treatment. Some medical schools devote little time to the study of tropical diseases. Internists generally are too busy trying to keep up with the latest findings on domestic diseases to worry about far-flung outbreaks and treatments. And while they might have some of the inoculation basics on hand they probably won't have everything you need in stock.

A travel clinic's physicians will have up-to-date information and know what you'll need based on where you're going, the time of year, and what you'll be doing. Make it clear to the doctor that you are not going on a relatively sterilized drive-by of the typical tourist sights, but that you'll be out in the countryside, Peace Corps–style, among the people, in their homes and villages. Travel to rural areas for extended periods requires some vaccinations and prophylactic drugs that typical tourist travel does not.

The travel clinic should provide the following:
- the immunizations you'll need
- an official "International Certificate of Vaccination" with all your immunizations recorded
- information on the preventive measures you should take to stay healthy
- prescriptions, such as one for the antimalarial that works best for the region you'll be visiting

NEXT STOP: YOUR FAMILY DOCTOR

Check with your family doctor, too. Let him or her know where you'll be going—how far, how high, and how fast. Make sure you're "all systems go"—for both your pretrip conditioning program and for the trek itself. You might have to doctor yourself in a medical emergency, so ask for some "just-in-case" prescriptions, including:
- broad-spectrum antibiotics (to fight respiratory or intestinal infections)

- an antidiarrheal drug
- a pain killer such as Tylenol No. 3 (with codeine)
- needles and syringes
- other prescriptions to meet specific needs (see "A Portable ER," below)

Ask your doctor to fill out a card with all your pertinent medical information (if you join IAMAT, they'll send you a passport-size medical-record card your doctor can use). Information should include any emergency medical data, conditions such as diabetes or allergies, drugs you might need, and drugs you should avoid. (Ask your doctor to use the understood-around-the-world generic names for drugs.) If you become sick or injured, a foreign doctor can check this card for your critical history.

Have your doctor check your medical records to see that your "childhood" shots are up to date; some might require boosters (see "A Shot In the Arm," below).

Ask your doctor about your current medications: Will any of them react with those prescribed for your trip? Will any interfere with your body's ability to cool off when you're exercising in heat and humidity? Will any of your trip's emergency drugs increase your sensitivity to the sun? Will they increase the rate at which your body loses water?

A SHOT IN THE ARM

SOME SERIOUS DISEASES—INCLUDING MALARIA, cholera, typhoid, rabies, dengue fever, hepatitis A, and hepatitis B—have managed to stake a claim in third world regions. In addition to these ubiquitous threats, most destinations offer their own unique pathogens. The incidence of many diseases is greater in remote areas, and the potential for exposure rises with activities such as meeting local people and visiting their homes. In other words, the places you'll be going and the things you'll be doing might increase your risk.

TIP

Needles and syringes could cause hassles at border crossings—but they could also be a lifesaver. They're in short supply in many developing countries, so they're often reused without proper sterilization. The needles or syringes a remote clinic might use on you could be contaminated with HIV or hepatitis B.

FOR WOMEN ONLY

Miles from nowhere is no place to get a urinary tract infection you can't treat. The same goes for a yeast infection—which could be triggered if you have to start taking one of those broad-spectrum antibiotics you brought along. Ask your doctor for a couple of prescriptions: an antibiotic for cystitis and the one-day oral medication for yeast infections.

TIP

If you're headed for mountains and you're sensitive to the effects of high altitude, a prescription for acetazolamide (Diamox) could help. Even if you're in great shape, you could get altitude sickness at relatively low levels. Youth and fitness aren't the determining factors—your personal susceptibility is, and it can't be predicted without experience.

TIP

Before you get your prescriptions filled, make two copies of each order to take with you on your trip. This paperwork could be helpful if questions arise as to why you're carrying certain drugs and paraphernalia.

You'll be many miles and often many days from emergency rooms and infectious-disease specialists, so you need to do everything you can to prevent infection, both before you leave and while you're traveling.

It's important to get started on your immunizations as early as possible. The days when you could get all your shots at the last minute are long gone. Some immunizations require a series of shots over more than six months.

At your initial visit to the travel clinic, sit down with your travel advisor and make a schedule that ensures you'll get all your shots in plenty of time, especially those that might cause a reaction. Many immunizations require two or more injections, and since you might need about six different shots, you'll have to plan carefully to space them safely. Moreover, with some immunizations it takes as long as four weeks after the last shot in the series to develop immunity.

Adventure travelers headed to remote regions in Asia, Africa, or Latin America will need some of the following vaccines, depending on their destination:

- **Yellow fever.** There's no drug to treat infection with this hemorrhagic virus, so a vaccination is crucial. Moreover, proof of vaccination is required for entry to several African and South American countries: If you don't have it, you run the risk not only of contracting the disease but of being stopped at the border or getting the shot from border guards equipped with questionable vaccine and syringes. Only a state-authorized, special travel clinic should give this immunization and sign your official vaccination card. The single dose becomes effective in ten days and is good for ten years.

- **Typhoid.** This bacterium is spread by food and water contaminated by fecal matter. It causes an intestinal infection with fever, headache, fatigue, loss of appetite, constipation, and other gastrointestinal symptoms. Capsules have replaced shots. The oral vaccine is taken every other day for four doses.

- **Hepatitis A.** This highly contagious liver disease is another one spread by fecal contamination of food and water. It causes pain, jaundice, weakness, and vomiting—enough to keep you in bed, perhaps hospitalized, for weeks or months. The old preventive was one or more gamma globulin shots, but the hepatitis A vaccine has made those obsolete. A single shot provides four weeks of protection—and don't forget, the clock starts ticking when you get the shot, not when you get on the plane! For longer protection, you need two shots—the second one six months after the first.

- **Hepatitis B.** Since this viral liver infection is commonly spread by sexual contact and infected needles, you might not think you need the vaccine. Much less likely but still possible, however, is transmission through contact with infected people who have open sores. (On a typical adventure travel trip you might find yourself shaking hands with a village chieftain and playing patty-cake with a child.) The vaccine consists of three shots, the second a month after the first, the third given five months after that. The immunity conferred lasts indefinitely.

- **Meningococcal meningitis.** This infection spreads through droplets from sneezes and coughs and inflames the linings of the brain and spinal cord. Severe cases begin with chills, headache, vomiting, and stiff neck—followed by convulsions, coma, and death. The vaccine comes in a single dose, and the immunity lasts at least three years. There also are other bacteria that can cause meningitis, for which vaccines are available.

- **Rabies.** This viral infection is invariably fatal without postexposure injections. Wild dogs and other animals are more of a risk in the rural areas of many developing countries, and they can spread infection through scratches or possibly just a lick. There is no vaccine that confers immunity, but a pretrip inoculation series can buy you enough time to be evacuated to a medical facility for a reduced number of postexposure shots. The pretrip series consists of three shots, the second one week after the first, and the third two or three weeks later.

- **Plague.** This bacterium is carried by fleas that have bitten infected rodents—usually rats, but also ground squirrels and other animals. It causes fever, headache, and painful lymph nodes. Without treatment it can cause potentially fatal blood and lung infections. Plague is treated with tetracycline, but if the vaccine is recommended you'll need three shots, each about four weeks apart, followed by two boosters six months apart.

• **Japanese B encephalitis.** Cases range from a flulike illness with headache and fever to very serious brain swelling. This disease is prevalent in some areas at certain times of the year. You must carefully weigh the risk of the disease against potential problems with the injections—some people have had severe allergic reactions—so if you get vaccinated you should remain close to medical care for several days after each shot. The vaccine is given in three doses, the second in seven days and the third on day 14 or 28.

• **Influenza.** If you're going to the Southern Hemisphere between April and September, you'll be there during their winter flu season. Even if you had a shot in fall or winter you should consider getting another, as immunity lasts only about six months. Allow plenty of time for this one because the vaccine has to be specially ordered after our flu season is over.

• **"Childhood vaccines."** Your childhood shots didn't give you lifelong protection, so you should check to see if you're due for a booster for polio or tetanus and diphtheria. If you've never had chicken pox, you should receive the varicella vaccine. And if you haven't had measles or been vaccinated, you need the measles, mumps, and rubella (MMR) vaccine. If you were born after 1957, for optimal protection you should have two injections more than a month apart.

• **Tickborne encephalitis.** This is one disease you won't need to worry about if you're headed for Southeast Asia, Africa, or Latin America. But if you're traveling in the summer and plan to add on a trip to Europe, China, or the former Soviet Union—where you'll risk infection—you could obtain an effective vaccine in Europe.

You might be wondering why cholera shots aren't on this list, as there are periodic outbreaks of this intestinal infection in many developing countries. Doctors no longer rec-

---

TIP

Some immunizations should not be administered if you're even moderately ill, so something like a bout with the flu could wreak havoc with your schedule. Leave a little leeway in your timing so you'll be able to finish everything before the last minute.

TIP

If you'll be taking the antimalarial drug chloroquine or mefloquine, you shouldn't schedule your last rabies shot for the week before departure. The antimalarial might block the immune response to the vaccine.

TIP

Not all immunizations come with a 100-percent guarantee. Some might give you only limited protection. The odds will be in your favor, but you'll still need to take precautions—which you should be taking anyway to guard against the other diseases out there.

TIP

If you're 65 or older, you're due for the pneumococcal vaccine even if you're not going abroad—so don't leave home without this one.

ommend the vaccine because it's not very effective: Only about half of those vaccinated develop immunity, and their immunity lasts only a few months. (Ask your doctor for an official-looking document that exempts you from cholera injections in case of trouble at a border crossing.)

ARTHROPOD AGONIES

THEY'RE OUT THERE WAITING FOR YOU: MOSQUITOES; KISS-ing bugs; lice; fleas; sand, black, and tsetse flies; gnats and midges; and many more arthropod threats. They carry myriad diseases in popular adventure travel regions.

Contact the Centers for Disease Control (see pages 158–159) for your destination's current threats and available treatments. Despite your willingness to offer up your flesh to needles, there is no vaccine for any of the diseases in the sampling that follows. And in many cases there's only limited treatment—no magic-bullet antibiotic.

Here are some of the threats and the areas where they're prevalent:

- **Chagas' disease (South and Central America).** This is caused by a parasite in the feces of the kissing bug, which infests mud and thatch buildings. Fever is an early symptom, sometimes followed by heart disease and enlarged intestines.
- **Sleeping sickness (Africa).** A bite from a tsetse fly can cause infection with this parasite. A sore similar to a boil forms at the site of the bite several days afterward. Severe illness occurs months later, with fever, swollen lymph nodes, and possible central nervous system problems. One strain—with cardiac involvement and rapid weight loss—can be fatal.
- **Dengue fever (Latin America).** This virus is common in tropical and subtropical regions. It's spread by mosquitoes, usually during or just after the rainy season. Joint and muscle pain can be so severe that the disease is often called "breakbone fever." In its milder form it's like the flu, but in serious cases there's high fever, blinding headaches, wracking chills, and months of exhaustion. Some cases can be fatal, with internal bleeding that fills the lungs and intestines.
- **Chikungunya fever (Africa, Indian subcontinent, Southeast Asia).** This mosquitoborne viral

infection causes fever, nausea, rash, headache, and joint pain, with stiffness sometimes lasting for months.

- **Filariasis (Central and South America, Africa, Indian subcontinent, Southeast Asia).** This parasite spread by mosquitoes causes the gross enlargement of the legs called elephantiasis.
- **Leishmaniasis (Central and South America, Africa, Indian subcontinent, Southeast Asia).** Courtesy of the sand fly, this parasite causes fever, weakness, skin sores, swollen spleen, and, in severe cases, destruction of facial tissue.
- **Congo-Crimean hemorrhagic fever (Central Asia, Indian subcontinent, Africa, Eastern Europe).** Ticks spread this one, which comes on suddenly with fever, headaches, chills, aches, and severe arm and leg pain. Fatal internal bleeding might occur.

MALICIOUS MALARIA

A parasitic infection transmitted by the *Anopheles* mosquito, malaria is one of the most serious—and ubiquitous—threats to adventure travelers. It starts with fever, chills, headache, nausea, muscle aches, and malaise. Malaria victims report renewed attacks with a ghastly array of agonies: drenching sweats, painful light sensitivity, insomnia, loss of appetite, and frightening delusions. Without treatment, malaria can lead to anemia, kidney failure, and in some cases even coma and death. It kills hundreds of thousands each year in Asia, Africa, South America, and the South Pacific.

Although there is no malaria vaccine, there are antimalarial drugs. But malaria has developed resistance to some drugs, and you and your doctor need to pinpoint the currently effective drug for the region you're going to. The two most common antimalarial drugs are chloroquine and mefloquine. Chloroquine has been used since World War II and side effects are rare. But in many areas the malaria parasite has become resistant to chloroquine. Mefloquine, commonly known as Lariam, is prescribed for travelers going to the increasing number of regions with chloroquine-resistant parasites. It is highly effective, but some users report unusual and alarming side effects such as hallucinations, convulsions, and depression. Anyone with a history of epilepsy or psychiatric problems should discuss its use with a physician.

Before using Lariam, or going to a destination where this antimalarial is the only effective option, you should become an informed consumer. Ultimately, it's like so many other decisions about adventure travel—a matter of considering the odds, the risks, and the benefits.

The dose for both chloroquine and mefloquine is one tablet per week, starting one week before entering the risky area and continuing for four weeks after leaving. It's best to start your dose on a Sunday, since your trip leader will probably follow the diplomatic and Peace Corps regimen of taking antimalarials on the first day of the week and will issue a reminder. It's much easier to take your dose on time if you're in synch with the rest of the group.

Doxycycline is an antibiotic that is sometimes prescribed as a substitute for mefloquine. This drug might increase your sun sensitivity, so if you are taking it you should be sure to pack a broad-brim hat, long-sleeved shirt, pants, and a strong sun block.

> **FOR WOMEN ONLY**
>
> Doxycycline is one of those antibiotics that sometimes kill beneficial bacteria, including those that keep yeast infections in check.

There are two other antimalarials you should know about. Proguanil is not available in the United States, but it can be purchased in Canada, Europe, and in many African countries. In some regions it's recommended as a supplement to be taken along with chloroquine. Side effects are relatively uncommon.

Fansidar was once prescribed as an antimalarial but is now recommended only in emergencies because of the potential for dangerous side effects, including allergic reactions. But if chloroquine turns out to be your antimalarial, your travel doctor might issue a prescription for a three-tablet emergency dose of this sulfa drug. Some experts say if you're in an area of chloroquine-resistant malaria and develop a fever and other symptoms, you should take Fansidar if you're more than twenty-four hours away from competent medical care.

The risk of malaria varies not only from one country to another but also from region to region. When you ask your travel doctor for an antimalarial, you should be very specific about

- where you're going
- the elevations you'll be traveling in
- the time of year
- what you'll be doing

For instance, some Nepal trips take groups from Himalayan ridges to jungle game parks. In the high country your risk is low, but you'll need an antimalarial from the 2,000-foot level on down. And on trips to many malaria-prone areas you'll be outdoors at dusk and dawn—the best times for bird spotting and wildlife watching—which is just when the mosquitoes are looking for their next meal.

The risk might also be higher if your visit follows on the heels of an exceptionally wet rainy season. For instance, in East Africa the recent El Niño downpours were followed by an outbreak of malaria.

OUNCES OF PREVENTION

You can't count on your antimalarial drug for 100-percent protection, so you need to ward off *Anopheles.* And you need to gird yourself against all those other arthropod agonies transmitted by insects and ticks. In much of the third world you should view insects as your mortal enemies. Draw up several lines of defense:

- Take plenty of heavy-duty insect repellent, one that contains at least 30 percent DEET. There are other insect repellents that are less toxic to you, but this is another case in which you have to weigh risks against benefits.
- Even in hot, humid areas you should cover your arms and legs. Clothes designed for the tropics are made of miracle fabrics and have air-conditioning vents that will keep you surprisingly comfortable. Elastic around wrists and ankles keeps intruders out.
- Nylon-mesh bug suits—tops and pants—keep bugs out and let air in. A mesh head net that fits over your hat will keep insects off your face and neck.
- Because the most dangerous mosquito period is dusk to dawn, a bed net or sleeping-bag net is a must. Even inside a room with screens, don't assume you're protected—there might be tiny holes or cracks. These sleeping nets come in lightweight models with multiple suspension options. Besides mosquitoes, they'll keep out bedbugs and assassin bugs as well.
- Permethrin is an insecticide that can be sprayed on clothing and netting, and it's safe for humans. It kills or repels insects on contact, and an application lasts two

weeks. Permethrin is biodegradable and won't cause stains or odors on your clothing.

OTHER WAYS TO GET SICK

THERE'S A BUNCH OF 'EM. FOOD- AND WATERBORNE DISEASES are the number-one cause of travel illness. They're in the soil and water in almost all primitive areas. They're also on the crops and in the livestock—which means that fruits, vegetables, and meats can all be contaminated. Moreover, they're on unwashed hands. Vaccines can protect you against some of the most serious ones (such as typhoid, polio, and hepatitis A), but you still need to be on guard against a host of viruses, parasites, and bacteria—including cholera.

Many of these cause the infamous "turista," or traveler's diarrhea. That can be debilitating—and mighty inconvenient —but it's seldom so severe that it becomes a serious medical problem. Some doctors advise antimotility drugs and early intervention with antibiotics. Rehydration and electrolyte replacement are important. Prompt medical attention might be required if you're in an area where there's been a cholera outbreak.

Parasites are insidious. They can cause an initial violent attack of diarrhea and cramps, then burrow in for the long haul and cause similar episodes for months after you return home. The testing to determine the specific cause and best treatment can be long and unpleasant.

Your adventure travel company's staff's most important job is to keep you safe and healthy. They should be providing sterilized water and serving food that has been scrupulously cleaned and prepared. For group meals there usually will be a hand-washing/disinfecting routine required before you pass through the food line.

When you're on your own wandering about a village or a town, it will be up to you to take precautions against contaminated food and drinks. (See Chapter 10, page 129, for more details.)

YOUR PORTABLE ER

AT TIMES YOU MIGHT BE DAYS AWAY FROM MEDICAL CARE, SO be prepared to doctor yourself in an emergency. Get those prescriptions from your family doctor and your travel specialist and assemble your own first-aid kit as well. Even though your trip leader should have first-aid training and extensive supplies, he or she might not always be close enough to give you immediate help for an injury.

The contents of your customized medical kit will depend on how rugged and how remote your trip will be. Here are some items to consider:

- **Foot care.** Moleskin (to prevent blisters); "second skin" gel pads (to treat the blisters you might get anyway); antifungal powder
- **First aid.** Triple antibiotic ointment; bandage strips; gauze squares (small, medium, large); tape; baby syringe (to flush a wound with sterilized water); antiseptic towelettes; elastic bandage (for ankle or knee); butterfly strips (to close a wound); safety pins; cotton swabs
- **Daily protection.** SPF 30 sunscreen (with both UVA and UVB protection)—an "all-day" waterproof brand that's PABA and fragrance free; insect repellent (30 percent DEET); lip balm with sunscreen protection; Permethrin (if your trip will outlast the two-week protection you get from treating your clothing and netting before you leave home)
- **Water purification.** Tablets plus flavoring to mask the iodine taste. (Some tablets such as Potable Aqua with PA Plus have a built-in flavor enhancer. If you get the plain iodine tablets, take along powdered lemonade and pour about a quarter-teaspoonful in your quart canteen—just enough to mask the bitter taste. Use the lemonade with artificial sweetener so you're not carrying the extra weight of all that sugar.)
- **Over-the-counter medications.** Acetaminophen (the pain reliever in Tylenol); an anti-inflammatory pain reliever such as ibuprofen; oral rehydration packets; cortisone cream or Benadryl spray; a sleep aid such as Sominex; chewable cough tablets; an anti-diarrheal such as Imodium A-D; a laxative; a motion-sickness preventive such as Dramamine; an oral antihistamine for mild to moderate allergic reactions; Pepto-Bismol tablets
- **Vitamins, herbs, and spices.** Chewable vitamin C (or echinacea) if you use that to beef up your immune system; lactobacillus capsules to keep your gastrointestinal system in order; a little picnic container of salt for emergency rehydration

- **Prescriptions.** Any normal daily medications (enough for your entire trip plus a one-week delay); antibiotics for respiratory and intestinal infections; penicillin (for tooth abscesses and as a prophylactic if you normally need it for procedures such as dental visits); antibiotic eye ointment; an antiviral drug to suppress viral infection symptoms; Tylenol No. 3 (Tylenol with codeine) for pain relief in case of something like a broken bone (best to have a doctor's letter next to this pill bottle). In addition to these general medications, there are some that are specific to certain regions, activities, and conditions: antimalarial medication; tetracycline for plague; scopolamine patches to fight motion sickness; epinephrine in a syringe if you're prone to a life-threatening allergic reaction to food or bee stings; acetazolamide (Diamox) to alleviate altitude sickness symptoms. Some doctors will also give prescriptions for dire-emergency treatments: dexamethasone for cerebral edema at very high altitudes; Fansidar in case malaria symptoms crop up when you're in a remote area at least twenty-four hours from expert medical care. (Note: Both dexamethasone and Fansidar have potentially serious side effects.)
- **Equipment.** Thermometer (so you'll know if you really have a fever); tweezers (for splinters and ticks); tiny scissors (if you didn't get a pocketknife with this feature)
- **Treatment information.** A portable wilderness-medicine handbook or photocopied pages; directions for all your antibiotics (you might be carrying more than one antibiotic, so it's important to match your symptoms to the right medication); information on all other drugs, including over-the-counter medications, with both generic and trade names, usage indications, dosages, precautions, side effects, interactions, and possible problems with altitude, alcohol, or sun
- **Phone numbers.** Your IAMAT list of English-speaking doctors; name, policy number, and phone number of your medical/evacuation insurance company; phone numbers (including evening/weekend) for U.S. embassy and consulates
- **Vocabulary words.** A card with a few key medical words and phrases translated: *pain; broken; fever; chills;*

TIP

Iodine tablets don't stay effective forever, so buy a fresh bottle from a camping store.

TIP

Ask your pharmacist to put all your prescriptions in the smallest possible pill vials and label with both trade and generic names. Keep your pills in their original containers—and wrap each vial with a folded copy of the prescription, using a rubber band to hold it on.

TIP

High altitudes sometimes cause antihistamine side effects, such as a rapid heartbeat. In thinner air, avoid anything containing codeine—such as a cough suppressant or Tylenol No. 3—because it might slow your breathing too much. Read the fine print before you pack so you'll know when and where you should take any medication—and tape a warning label over the tops of the containers.

TIP

Is there something medical personnel should know about you immediately—a medical condition, allergies, or a daily medication? You might want to wear a bracelet or dog tag with that information engraved on it. (Or you could join an organization such as Medic Alert, which keeps your critical facts on file, plus phone numbers for your doctor and family. They issue a tag or bracelet with your essential information, personal ID number, and their twenty-four-hour "call collect" phone number. For contact information see the Appendix, page 159.)

sore. And just in case you don't like the looks of the medical help you're about to get and would rather wait until you're evacuated: *no thanks; don't use; no injection; no anesthesia; no surgery*

- **Medical record.** A copy of your official International Certificate of Vaccination (staple the original to the inside back cover of your passport); vital details such as your blood type; current medications (generic names); and allergies
- **Needles and syringes.** Depending on where you live, you might need a prescription for these. Keep them in their original wrappers, along with a letter from your doctor authorizing you to carry them. A "stitch kit" also is good to have—in case you get a deep cut, you can get (or give yourself) a sterile mending job.
- **Traveler's dental kit.** Fillings can come loose—often at the worst times. These kits contain a temporary filling mix and a topical anesthetic to relieve the pain.

NEVER TOOTH SOON

EVEN IF YOUR TRIP IS JUST A GLEAM IN YOUR eye, make an appointment with your dentist for a thorough checkup, including X rays. If your teeth are intact there won't be any need for preventive work, but if you have several old fillings you might be a candidate for an overseas toothache.

Over the years, fillings can shrink and leak, allowing bacteria to penetrate the pulp and cultivate serious infection. If your dentist sees trouble like this brewing, consider going ahead with the repair work before you go, even if it's not absolutely necessary at the time. If you've ever had an abscess, you know what one could do to your trip of a lifetime; if you haven't, you don't want to find out far from home.

Replacing obsolescent fillings can be a multiweek process, especially if molar cavities and crowns are involved. So allow plenty of lead time for this pretrip preparation. Even if you do get preventive work done it's still a good idea to get a prescription for penicillin from your dentist—in case an infection pops up in an unexpected spot while you're traveling. The antibiotic might keep the infection under control until you get back to your dentist.

CHAPTER 6

GETTING FIT TO GO

DURING YOUR PRETRIP MONTHS, YOUR EXERCISE SCHEDule is just as important as your vaccine schedule. You need to build strength and stamina—and minimize your chances of injury. It's time to tailor a fitness regimen to make sure you're prepared for the physical challenges ahead.

In the fine print in some catalogs there's a clause stating that the trip leader has the right to jettison you in the middle of the trip (with no refund for your unused portion) if he or she thinks you're not fit enough to keep up with the group. That sort of dramatic exit is a rarity, but this clause emphasizes the fact that you need to devote serious—and prompt—attention to a fitness regimen.

Adventure travel trips run the gamut from "easy" trips (such as floating down the lazy Amazon River) to "strenuous" treks (such as crossing the 16,000-foot Cordillera Blanca). Chances are if you fit the profile for either end of the spectrum, you know who you are.

You know your strengths and your limitations. If you take regular walks you're probably ready for the easy trip; if you're considering the second type you probably lift weights, run miles, and do all the other things the very fit do to keep their strength up and their heart rate down.

But there's a big range between these extremes, and most adventure trips fall somewhere in the middle. Some companies label this middle ground "moderate," while others that use a number-ranking system rate these a II or a III on a scale from I to V.

Your challenge is to pick a trip you're capable of—or one you can get ready for by departure time if you put in a few months of faithful conditioning.

Companies vary widely in their concept of what's needed in terms of fitness for their moderate trips. One company simply says you won't have a problem with its moderate trips if you're in good health. Another says you'll need to be ready to walk for about six hours a day on mountainous terrain up to 14,000 feet—which takes a lot more than what most people consider good health.

If you're not already a hiker, it might be hard to judge the difficulty of a trip that involves moderate (II to III) walking. If you can walk on your city sidewalks you can walk on some trails right now. And you probably can walk for as *long* on a trail as you can on a sidewalk—but likely not nearly as *fast* or as *far*.

If you're a newcomer to this type of active travel, it's better to underestimate rather than overestimate your ability. A company might rate a trip involving three hours of walking per day at lower elevations easy to moderate (and it would be, by adventure travel standards). So you might think, "No problem, I can take a three-hour walk any day."

But three hours on a sea-level city sidewalk or rail trail is not the equivalent of three hours of climbing from 6,000 feet to 8,000 feet—which is still a "lower" elevation by Himalayan or Andean standards. Putting one foot in front of the other on flat terrain is easy, but doing the same thing in thin air on a steep and rocky slope can be grueling.

To give you some idea of how much harder it is to go up hills, here is the general guideline used in hiking books to let people know how long and how hard a hike is from point A to point B: *Allow a half hour for each mile and another half hour for each 1,000 feet of elevation gain.* For example, an eight-

TIP

If you've never hiked and are within driving distance of terrain that has elevation gains of at least a thousand feet, go out and try this sort of walking. See how you measure up to the general timing guidelines. It will give you some idea of how well you'd be able to keep up with your group—and how much extra conditioning you'll need.

mile hike in which you climb from 3,000 to 5,000 feet will take about five hours—and that's without stops for gazing or grazing. And on routes at higher altitudes—starting at about 8,000 feet, where most people start to feel the effects of thinner air—ascents are slower and tougher.

You can't assume that going down will be much easier. On a steep, rocky descent, where each step involves balancing on a slanted surface, you can't just let gravity take over and do the work for you. On rough terrain, the guideline above applies to descents as well.

STEP UP TO A TEST

ONE MAJOR ADVENTURE TRAVEL COMPANY'S CATALOG offered a concrete way to assess your fitness level and your readiness for one of its treks—the Harvard Step Test.

If you're about five feet nine inches tall, you'll need a step that's sixteen inches high; if you're much shorter or taller, use one that's proportionally lower or higher. Step up and down for four minutes, alternating your feet at a thirty-times-per-minute pace. Then sit quietly and count your heartbeats for thirty seconds at three intervals: one minute, two minutes, and three minutes after you stopped exercising. Add these three pulse counts. Double that figure (call this the pulse count total). Then compute your "recovery index": Divide 24,000 (which is the number of seconds you exercised times 100) by your pulse count total.

For example, after four minutes (240 seconds) of exercise followed by one minute of rest, your pulse count for thirty seconds is 80. After two minutes of rest your pulse count is 60. After three minutes of rest your pulse count is 50.

$$80 + 60 + 50 = 190$$
$$190 \times 2 = 380 \text{ (your pulse count total)}$$
$$24,000 \div 380 = 63.2 \text{ (your recovery index score)}$$

This test grades your heart's recovery rate. The better your conditioning, the higher your score. The travel company described above says you need to score in the high 60s to have a good chance of successfully participating in one of its moderate treks.

HOW MUCH DO YOU NEED TO TRAIN?

YOU'LL SEE A WIDE RANGE IN WHAT COMPANIES SAY IS necessary in pretrip training for a moderate trip.

Some companies say you simply need to do some sort of aerobic exercise—such as bicycling or brisk walking—for thirty minutes a day, six days a week. But this might not be enough for some moderate trips.

Other companies say you need to make a special effort to get in top physical condition, doing heavy-breathing, break-a-sweat aerobic exercise well beyond your normal routine. This makes sense—after all, your energy expenditures on your trip will most likely be well beyond your normal weekly exercise regimen in terms of both time and distance.

And some companies suggest you start augmenting your normal fitness routine at least three months before departure—but preferably even further ahead of time. Giving yourself less time than that will be cutting it too close and won't allow for time-outs for sick days or business trips.

If you need to reserve your place on a trip far in advance, but your physical condition doesn't match the trip rating, ask yourself some key questions and be brutally honest with your answers:

- Is there enough time before departure to get in shape?
- Am I able to stick to a healthy eating regimen?
- Have I ever stuck to an exercise program long enough to get substantial results?
- Have I been in good enough shape to do this trip within the last year or so? Ever?
- Will I have enough extra time in the months ahead for exercise and training activities?
- How hard am I willing to work?
- And, the nitty-gritty question: How hard will I *really* work?

> **TIP**
>
> Unless you're superfit and extremely active, you might be better off opting for a trip that's a notch below what you think you can do. The landscape, culture, and wildlife will be so absorbing and so exhilarating that even if you've underestimated your capability for that trip, you won't be antsy if you don't get your quota of aerobic exercise.

FROM DESK JOCKEY TO ADVENTURE ATHLETE

PADDLING TRIPS REQUIRE UPPER-BODY STRENGTH, STRONG swimming skills, and confidence in the water. Trekking or bicycling in any hilly region requires strong legs and lungs. They all require endurance and cardiovascular fitness.

If you want to have a good time and move along effortlessly (or as close to it as possible when you're going up those hills) you need to get your lungs in shape. If you do, they'll send a steady flow of oxygenated blood to fuel your muscles when you're off on your adventure.

If you don't engage in some sort of aerobic exercise already, start now. Outdoors, you can walk briskly, jog, bicycle, or cross-country ski. Indoors, you can use the treadmill, exercise bike, stair climber, or cross-country skiing or rowing machines.

To make sure you're working hard enough you need to get your heart working at 60 to 90 percent of your maximum rate. There's a broad, generalized formula you can use to figure this out: Subtract your age from 220; multiply that number by .9 for the high end and by .6 for the low end of your "target range." Do some sort of aerobic exercise to get your heart rate up into this range for twenty to thirty minutes, six times a week.

If you've let your exercise regimen slide or if you've been a casual stroller rather than a brisk walker, check with your doctor before you begin serious aerobic training. You might need to lower your target range, at least at first. Here's how to gauge if you're working hard but not too hard: You should be breathing hard but still able to talk.

PRACTICE RUNS

The best preparation for your trip is what fitness experts call *specificity training*. Whatever your trip's main activity is, train for it by doing that as much as possible.

In good weather on the weekends, make the effort to get to some place where you can do whatever trip activity you've chosen. Take an all-day hike or bike ride on Saturday, then do it again on Sunday. Put in the miles; push yourself to do more than you usually do. It's important to do this at least two days in a row. After all, on your trip you won't be able to recuperate with a couch-potato Sunday after one day of hard trekking or pedaling. The more you simulate your trip activity, the better off you'll be when you actually do it. Hard work now will minimize the pain and strain when you're on your trek.

On most trips the "active exploration" involves walking or hiking (which is really just walking longer distances, often up and down slopes). So get out there and walk—up and down hills, up and down stairs—as often as you can during the week. Use the stair climber and the treadmill at the gym at night. On weekends, if you live close to any mountains, go on hikes where you gain 2,000 to 3,000 feet of elevation before you turn back to your car.

One of the great features of most treks is the service. You won't have to carry any of your gear except what you'll need during the day—porters, Sherpas, yaks, or llamas will do it for you. If you're going beyond the realm of inns and lodges, they'll carry tents, food, sleeping bags, and cooking utensils as well. But the weight of your daypack alone might surprise you.

So on your weekend training hikes, don't blithely stroll along with only a sandwich and water bottle. Try to approximate the conditions of a typical day on your adventure travel hike. Carry a daypack weighted down with your camera, extra lenses, lunch, snack bars, first-aid kit, rain gear, and an extra layer of clothing. Water weighs eight pounds per gallon, and you'll probably want to have at least two quarts with you when you're trekking.

It all adds up to a small monkey on your back. That pack now weighs enough to slow you down a little. If you'll be hiking a few thousand feet higher than your practice hikes, put at least another gallon of water in your pack so the extra weight will simulate the difficulty of using your lungs and muscles in thinner air.

Do the same sort of specificity training if you'll be paddling or cycling. Put in some long hours on the weekends doing the real thing. During the week, concentrate on the rowing machine or the exercise bike.

THE ALTITUDE FACTOR

If you're going trekking high in the mountains, your cardiovascular fitness is doubly important. At 10,000 feet you'll be taking in about 30 percent less oxygen than at sea level. If you're not in shape, your lungs will be bursting and your legs burning when you get up into that thinner air. It won't feel good, you won't have fun, and you'll have trouble keeping up with the group.

Training on a flat surface simply won't do. If you live out on the prairie, you'd better do a lot of stair climbing.

> **TIP**
>
> Get into the habit of wearing a weighted daypack during the week while you're walking hills or climbing stairs. It will speed your conditioning and get you used to carrying that extra load.

> **IT HAPPENED**
>
> When the group assembled for a ten-day "moderate" Alpine traverse, about half were wearing T-shirts from marathons they'd run. "Uh-oh," thought some of the others, mere hikers who thought they would have trouble keeping up with those runners. Yet when it came to huffing and puffing up and over the high passes, those who walked up and down hills regularly did better than some of those runners from the flat Midwest.

BREAKING IN YOUR BOOTS

If you need new hiking boots for your trip, buy them early and start wearing them, first around the house, then on walks. Wear them on your way to the office every day—and get off the bus or subway a stop or two sooner and walk those extra blocks. Your goal: to break those boots to bedroom-slipper comfort before you leave the country.

Wearing your new boots to work, on shopping trips, and around the neighborhood is great, but you need to check out how compatible your boots and your feet will be after a long day's march. Give them some specificity training as well: Take at least three ten-mile hikes in your new boots well before departure time—more if possible.

BUILDING MUSCLE STRENGTH

If you don't already work out on weight machines, start now. By departure time you'll have bigger, stronger muscles to go with your cardiovascular fitness. Exercises such as sit-ups, pull-ups, push-ups, and abdominal crunches are great, but try to use weight machines or free weights to really build muscles fast. To make progress, use weights three times a week, but only every other day—your muscles need an interval to rest and heal.

COFFEE BREAK WORKOUTS

With a busy schedule, it's hard to find enough time for exercise during the week, especially if you need to increase your regimen to prepare for a trip. But you can accomplish a lot at your office during your work day. Just use those spare minutes and a nearby chair or wall to boost your fitness. You won't need any fancy equipment or a complete change of clothes—just a T-shirt, ankle weights, running shoes, and a new mindset that takes advantage of phone times and coffee breaks.

Normally, when you finish a project you probably stretch, look out the window, maybe get a cup of coffee, or head down the hall for a little office gossip. Instead, use those opportunities to do some quick exercising. Miniworkouts interspersed throughout your normal work day can do surprising things for your muscle strength and aerobic fitness. The best news: You can do many of these exercises while you're talking on the phone (even more if you have a speaker phone).

Strengthening Your Legs: Your legs propel you across landscapes, up hills, over mountains. Whether you'll be walking or bicycling, the stronger those leg muscles the better your trip.

On a trekking trip you'll stress your knees and ankles, especially on steep grades and uneven terrain. Strong leg muscles will stabilize these joints, power you on ascents, and steady you on descents. You can do a lot in your office to increase flexibility, build strength, and reduce your chances of injury.

Work on your quadriceps so those upper thigh muscles will get you up hills and hold your knees in place on the downhills. Here are three great exercises:

- Sit on your chair and straighten one leg. Flex your foot, pulling your toes toward you. Lift your entire leg off your chair. Hold for ten to twenty seconds, then do the other leg. Continue until the phone conversation ends.
- Get those ankle weights out of the bottom file drawer and strap them on. Sit in your desk chair and straighten and slowly raise your lower leg until it's horizontal with the floor. Hold for a count of five and slowly lower.
- Maybe you should shut your door for this one: Stand with your back against the wall. Slowly slide your back down the wall until your thighs are horizontal with the floor. You should look as if you're sitting in an imaginary chair. Hold this pose until your thigh muscles quiver and burn—at least one minute, and longer if you can.

In-office calf exercises will increase your uphill strength and help prevent an ankle sprain that could leave you disabled in the middle of your trip. Try these:

- Kick off your shoes and stand on a fat phone book with your heels hanging off the edge. Rise up on your tiptoes, then lower your heels. Repeat fifteen to twenty times.
- Sit at your desk and lift one heel while pressing down hard on your toes. Hold for about five to ten seconds, then lower.

Back and Arms: If you're going on a paddling trip, the need for strong arm muscles is obvious. But even if you're trekking, upper-body strength is important. Do these exercises on quick breaks:

- You don't have to get down on the floor to do push-ups. Stand about four feet away from the wall and lean toward it, putting your hands on the wall, shoulder-width apart. Keeping your elbows in toward your body, push off from the wall slowly until your arms are straight, then slowly lower your chest toward the wall.
- Or use your desk: Stand facing your desk, put your hands on the edge, and move your feet backward about three feet. Slowly lower your chest to the desk, then slowly push up, keeping your body in a straight line.
- Grasp a book or an ankle weight in each hand, arms at your sides. First, bend your elbows and bring the weights up to your shoulders in a bicep curl. After a few of those, raise your arms sideways (keep them straight) slowly to shoulder height.
- Sit with your feet on the floor and your palms on the arms of your chair. Slowly straighten your arms and raise yourself off your seat. Hold the pose for about ten seconds.
- Place two chairs (the kind without wheels!) about four feet apart, facing each other. Put your hands on the edge of one chair seat and your feet on the other chair. Lower yourself slowly between them, then lift your body until your elbows are straight.

Stairsteps to Fitness: Just outside your office door is the route to cardiovascular fitness. Change into a T-shirt, put on some running shoes, and duck out to your building's stairwell. While others fill up on Danish and gossip, you can run up a few flights of stairs. Just five minutes of this two or three times a day will pay big dividends.

If you haven't been running or power walking regularly, start slowly, going up and down just one flight of stairs at a comfortable pace. Then add flights and speed, so you're running up multiple flights and dashing down again. You should be able to go up and down one or more flights for a total of fifty in fifteen minutes—and that's for a slower paced trek.

After a few weeks, bring your daypack to the office. Load it with your ankle weights plus a phone book and wear it on your stairwell workouts.

Stretch Out Your Workout: As you build muscle you need to stay flexible as well. Warm up your muscles first and then stretch slowly, holding each stretch for about thirty seconds.

- Hamstrings: Lift one leg and put your heel on your desk. Reach out to that ankle and bend forward as far as you can.
- Calves and Achilles tendons: Stand about four feet from the wall. Lean forward and place your hands on it, keeping your back straight and your heels on the floor.
- Quadriceps: Stand on your left foot and grasp your right ankle with your left hand. Pull your foot gently toward your buttocks. Reverse legs.
- Arms: With your right hand, reach across your back and touch your left shoulder. Hold for twelve seconds, feeling the pull. Alternate arms.

FIT TO GO

The important thing is to approach this trip like an athlete in training. Don't lapse, and don't get lazy. (Well, you can slack off occasionally on the weights, but not on the aerobic exercise.)

And don't make excuses! In bad weather, you still need to do your time—indoors, on a bike, stair climber, rowing machine, treadmill, or plain old flights of stairs.

CHAPTER 7

GEAR, CLOTHING, AND OTHER ESSENTIALS

YOU'LL BE WORKING HARD AT GETTING PHYSICALLY FIT for your adventure, but save time for some less strenuous exercise: strolling through stores or thumbing through catalogs. It will take a while to assemble all the right gear and outdoors clothing, so start shopping months before your departure date. And if you need hiking boots, put them first on your list so you'll have plenty of time to break them in properly.

THE EFFICIENT ADVENTURE TRAVELER

IF YOU'RE GOING ADVENTURE TRAVELING, YOU'LL NEED TO PACK much more selectively than if you were heading off to a resort or a cruise. Instead of throwing a fashionable wardrobe into a couple of jumbo suitcases, you'll have to round up an array of specialized clothing and equipment and stuff it all into a duffel and a daypack.

On an ordinary vacation trip your primary concern might be

style, but on an adventure travel trip your basic criteria are safety, comfort, and convenience. Without civilization's backstop, you'll need all sorts of gear that you'd never dream of taking on a trip to Disney World—and you'll need clothing that's designed to protect your body, not enhance your looks. Staying warm and dry is not only more comfortable, it's crucial in the extreme conditions you might encounter in the outback.

Here are some basic rules:

- Take only what you can carry yourself. Where you're going, you can't count on help, and besides, at times you might want to keep your gear secure in your own hands. Even for a three-week adventure travel trip, everything should fit into that daypack and duffel bag.
- Choose gear that's versatile: a watch-alarm; a calculator–translator–currency converter.
- Choose double-duty clothing: shorts (and sports bras) that double as swimwear; long underwear that doubles as pajamas.
- Look for items with lots of pockets: chest pockets, inside pockets, cargo pockets, deep pockets. They'll be like little file drawers for all sorts of small items such as film, lenses, minicamera, minibinoculars, insect repellent, tissues—all those little things that won't be so handy if they're stowed in your daypack.
- Pack light, but pack all the essentials. Follow the "what to pack" list provided by your adventure travel company. After reading this chapter, you might want to take some different or additional items, but in general you should follow their instructions. They've been there, done that, and know what you'll need.
- You won't have room for a fresh change of clothes each day. If you've been backpacking you already know you can get along in the same socks and underwear a few days in a row and still live with yourself. Just as with any camping trip, your companions will be in the same boat. A little scent among friends is acceptable.

DRESS FOR SUCCESS

Forget looking chic and sexy or fashionable and affluent. If you're dressed for the climate and culture, you'll have the savvy look that says you're a person who knows how to survive off the beaten path. And the more comfortable you are, the more you'll enjoy yourself. Follow these wardrobe guidelines:

- Choose clothes that won't show an accumulation of dirt.
- Bring items that will keep you cool, calm, and collected in steamy regions, and gear that will keep you warm and dry in cold and damp conditions. Be ready for big temperature swings, such as hot days and cold nights, or changes in altitude that mean shifts in climate zones.
- Plan to cope with these changes by adding or subtracting layers of clothing made of the new, lightweight, quick-dry, scrunchable, moisture-wicking, insulating synthetics, plus breathable rain gear.
- Opt for slightly oversized shirts and pants. They're more acceptable in many cultures than tight clothes. When it's hot they allow the air to circulate, and when it's chilly they leave room to add insulating layers underneath. Moreover, this clothing won't be revealing: You'll have no telltale bulge announcing the location of your travel wallet.

MATERIAL MATTERS

Just say no to cotton: Leave your beloved T-shirts and blue jeans at home. They might seem like down-home comfort, but they're not the best adventure travel partners. Cotton provides absolutely no warmth when wet, and even in warmer climes you can get chilled when the wind picks up. Moreover, it won't dry fast enough when you wash it.

Switch to nylon and polyester for your trip. A combination of tops and bottoms in high-tech versions of these fabrics will see you through the heat, cold, exertion, and rough terrain of any location and climate. These miracle fabrics are also light-weight and quick drying—perfect travel companions.

Nylon isn't always the slippery, shiny stuff of your old windbreakers. It's been reincarnated as Supplex and Nycott, fabrics that are surprisingly soft, like an old cotton broadcloth shirt next to your skin. It's superquick to dry and superlight to pack. Unlike cotton, high-tech nylon is one of the new breed of "wicking" fabrics that moves moisture away from your skin and disperses it over the outside surface of the fabric. That means you'll be less sticky in the heat and less clammy when you work up a sweat in cold weather.

The new polyester isn't your father's polyester. These new fabrics don't bear any resemblance to those 1970s knit suits, and they certainly don't act the same. The new, lightweight polyesters designed to keep you cool in hot weather have the look and feel of T-shirts. This quick-drying material also wicks away your sweat from your skin. The cold-weather fabrics come in a range of thickness, from polypropylene long underwear to microfleece to thick pile. All dry quickly and transfer moisture away from your skin.

Fleeces and piles have other bonuses: They're water resistant, soft, and tightly woven to block the wind. With tiny air pockets on their surface, they provide great insulation. And they keep you at least as warm as wool yet take up about half the space.

The sun's rays are often more intense at adventure travel destinations—shadeless deserts, equatorial climes, open waters, and mountain slopes. With conventional fabrics, covered up doesn't necessarily mean protected: A cotton T-shirt might have an SPF of only about 7, well below the level recommended by dermatologists. So even if you're wearing long sleeves and pants you could be getting too much ultraviolet radiation if you're in the sun all day. But shirts and pants made of the new Solumbra fabric offer 30+ SPF protection from both UVB and UVA rays (few sunscreens block the latter).

> **IT HAPPENED**
>
> Travelers in a Central American jungle washed their cotton broadcloth shirts and cotton knit briefs. Five days later everything was still too wet to wear or pack. Only the new synthetics would have dried in that steamy heat.

COLOR CALCULATIONS

Leave the hot magentas and the neon limes for the home turf. Neutral colors will allow you to blend in with the local crowds as much as possible. (And if you're headed for East Africa, you'll be less attractive to the tsetse fly, which is drawn by the movement of bright colors.) Another factor: If you tone it down, you'll look less like an American, which can be a distinct advantage in many places.

If not hot pink, then what? Prints disguise dirt, wrinkles, and food stains. In general, dark colors are good travelers, too, great at hiding accumulated dirt and grime. Black has enough of an elegant aura to get you from the outback to the opera with most of your aplomb intact. If your trip features a night on the town on the last day of the tour, or if you have a city stop planned on the way home, just tuck a scarf or a tie into your bag to make the transformation from wanderer to sophisticate.

TIP

While it might be a great hide-all-the-dirt print, don't bring hunting-style camouflage-pattern pants or shirts (the same goes for soldier-olive shades). In some countries, sporting a military look could get you more attention and excitement than you've bargained for.

But if you're headed to the desert or the tropics, you'll roast in the sun's hot rays if you're wearing dark colors. Take some pale shades that will reflect the sun. Opt for dusky hues—medium tan, smoke gray, moss green—that won't show dust.

Lighter colors have another advantage: If you're in tick territory it's easier to spot the creatures before they latch on to your skin.

And even in cooler climates, navy and black are a bad idea if the area is a prime mosquito habitat. These colors are like beacons to those bloodsuckers.

ADVENTURE APPAREL

CHOOSE FROM A COMBINATION OF THE FOLLOWING STYLES and fabrics based on your destination and planned activities.

INNERWEAR

- **Shirts.** The best are Supplex or Nycott nylon, long-sleeved, button-down-the front shirts with collars and patch pockets. A good choice for most places. In hot weather they will protect your arms and neck from sunburn and insect bites; a light color with a loose fit will still be cool, especially if you get a style with mesh panels on the back and under the arms.
- **Knit shirts.** Tank, short-sleeved, long-sleeved—whatever the temperature dictates. Look for those in a Cool-Max nylon/polyester blend with a T-shirt feel. Made of this evaporation-promoting fabric, they're cool in the heat and great for layering under long-sleeved button-fronts when it's chilly.
- **Microfleece.** Turtleneck, zippered mock-turtleneck, or collar-and-button-front styles are the best choices to layer on as the temperature drops. This synthetic fabric insulates, blocks wind, wicks away sweat, resists rain, but still keeps you warm even if wet. Let it snow, let it blow! Two layers (on top and bottom), plus long underwear, plus Gore-Tex outerwear will keep you comfortable in brutal conditions.
- **Pants.** For your primary pair, choose soft nylon, with lots of pockets and zip-off legs so you can convert to shorts if it warms up—then just zip the bottoms back on when it cools

down or when bare legs are inappropriate (such as entering a Muslim town). Look for ankle zippers that allow you to take off the legs without taking off your boots. For a second pair of pants (depending on your activities and destinations), look for such features as a gusseted crotch for more range of motion; elastic ankles to keep out insect invaders; lots of storage space, including cargo pockets and a zippered security pocket; microfleece for cold temperatures; sturdy canvas for tough conditions.

- **Nylon running or cycling tights.** Another good insulating layer; also good for wearing under shorts so your legs won't get scratched by briars. Could help on a strenuous trip: Studies show that tights slow the buildup of lactic acid in your muscles so you'll feel and perform better.

- **Shorts.** Look for nylon again, with mesh pockets for quick draining (ideal for any occasion when you might get drenched—paddling through waves, hiking through a tropical downpour, swimming in a lagoon). They'll dry very fast and eliminate the need to change in and out of swimwear. For a second pair, you might want sturdy canvas, with cargo pockets.

- **Underwear.** Briefs in the new polyester/Lycra blend feel soft, dry fast, and wick moisture away from your skin. Some even have an antimicrobial finish that keeps odors down, a big plus since you won't have room to pack fresh underwear for every day of your trip.

- **Long underwear.** Choose synthetic tops and bottoms. This insulating under layer is important when it's cold and can double as pajamas (which you might need, since adventure travelers often sleep in group accommodations—from village homes to mountain-hut dorms). These moisture-wicking, speed-dry poly-

---

FOR WOMEN ONLY

Long-sleeved nylon shirts come in women's sizes, but you might want to buy one in the men's section. Size small will fit all but petites. And there's an advantage to buying a man's shirt: better pockets.

FOR WOMEN ONLY

Long skirts are available in soft nylon, with deep pockets, button front, and elastic waists. These skirts are great in countries where it's important to show respect for the culture by not appearing in public in pants. On warm-weather treks, skirts are almost as cool as shorts but also protect your legs from the sun. And when it's cooler, you can wear tights under your skirt, in thicknesses ranging from nylon to microfleece depending on the temperature.

FOR WOMEN ONLY

When nature calls, you might find yourself on a treeless plain miles from anything resembling an outhouse—and no concealing brush or boulders. The longer length of a trekking skirt or man's shirt will provide a bit of pit stop privacy. And elastic waists on your pants and shorts will make such stops faster and easier.

FOR WOMEN ONLY

Pack sports bras made of moisture-wicking polyester with Spandex: They provide support for any activity and double as swimwear (with Supplex shorts). They dry fast, so you can go from raft to van without changing.

ester knits come in weights to match your needs—from chilly nights to icy peaks.

OUTERWEAR

- **Jacket.** Choose one constructed of a fabric such as Gore-Tex—windproof and waterproof yet breathable—so the moisture vapor from your skin can pass through and escape.
- **Windbreaker.** If you're positive you won't need waterproofing, this is a second choice to ward off cool winds and evening chills. The most versatile model has a hood hidden in the collar and fifteen pockets and sheds its sleeves to convert to a photographer's vest.
- **Travel vest.** Festooned with pockets, this style provides a great filing system: You'll have separate spaces for all sorts of items including film, lenses, lens cleaner, camera, binoculars, map, compass, notebook and pen, tissues and wipes, sunglasses, balaclava, moleskin, sunscreen, phrasebook. Whatever you'll need for the day is conveniently located with handy access.
- **Hats.** Hot or cold, wet or dry, you'll need to cover your head. Options include baseball cap (with extralong bill and an attachable back flap to shield your neck from the sun); Australian-outback style (with a broad brim all around to keep the sun or rain off your face and neck and a bolo-style leather strap so you won't lose it in the wind); balaclava (a three-way knit that serves as a neck warmer, hat, and face mask all in one; a lightweight model tucked away in a pocket is a great emergency head cover to have when you get chilled, since as much as 80 percent of your body's heat can escape through your bare head); knit hat (cozy when it's chilly, especially for sleeping; in really cold weather you can layer it with your balaclava underneath and your hood drawn tight on top); fleece visor (with sun-shielding brim and ear-warming flaps, it lets you vent heat off the top of your head when you're exercising hard in cold weather).

OPTIONS FOR HANDS AND FEET

- **Gloves.** Depending on conditions, you'll need lightweight Lycra or microfleece gloves; pile mittens; and/or water- and windproof overmitts.

- **Sports gloves.** You can prevent blisters with padded biking gloves or neoprene paddling gloves.
- **Boots.** Even if you're not going trekking, light- or medium-weight hiking boots are a good choice if you'll be doing any sort of active exploration on land. Sturdy, waterproof boots will keep your feet dry, cushion your soles, and support your ankles on everything from uneven cobblestones to rocky shores.

  If you need new boots, buy them far ahead of time. To make sure you get the right fit and the right boot, shop late in the day, when your feet have swollen from their morning size (and make sure your feet aren't cold); take a pair of thick hiking socks and a liner pair for sizing the boots. Go to a store where the sales staff also hike so you'll get the right model for the places you'll be going. Your boots should be heavy enough to give you the right support, but not too heavy—a pound on your feet is harder to carry than four pounds on your back. Be sure to follow the manufacturer's instructions on waterproofing.

  If you already have hiking boots, get a new pair of laces and give the leather a good treatment—waterproofing if necessary. For a paddling, bicycling, or horseback trip, follow your adventure travel company's recommendations for footwear.
- **Extra footwear.** You'll definitely want to slip your hard-working feet into something different at the end of the day. Running shoes are a good choice; so are sandals with cushioned soles. Sports sandals (the ones with gripper rubber soles and nylon straps) can do triple duty, from river running to relaxing to city touring. Shower thongs are good to have when you're faced with less-than-pristine facilities.
- **Socks.** More than just a go-between for your feet and your shoes, hiking socks have the right materials and construction to cushion your soles from rocks and shocks and keep your feet drier and warmer. The new synthetic fabrics also dry quickly. Since most adventure travel trips involve a lot of walking, do as hikers do and wear two pairs of socks: thin, breathable liner socks that wick away

> **TIP**
>
> Travelers to some hot and steamy areas report roaches "the size of mice." If you're headed for such a region, take an extra pair of old socks in a Ziploc bag. At night, whenever you're in a place with indoor plumbing, stuff one sock in the tub drain and the other in the sink drain to block off the entry points for these repulsive arthropods.

moisture (polypropylene, CoolMax, or Thermastat), and a thicker pair with a combination of synthetics, with perhaps a bit of cotton or wool (look for padding on the heel and ball of the foot, and also on the instep to buffer your foot from boot folds and lace pressure). Choose moisture-wicking fabrics that are the right thickness for your boot and the weather you expect. For instance, if you'll be trekking at higher altitudes where it will get cold, get thicker, winter-style socks that have more wool in the mix, especially at the toe.

SAFETY AND SURVIVAL GEAR

MOST ADVENTURE TRAVEL COMPANIES SEND THEIR CLIENTS pretrip packing lists. But don't count on your company to include all the safety and survival items you *should* take. Some of the items described below, such as a compass, might not be on your "official" packing list—but they could save your life in an emergency.

- **Compass, maps, and guidebook pages.** When you're on a trip with a leader, you're naturally inclined to relax and drink in the sights and scenery without worrying about whether you're on the right track. Nevertheless, it's a good idea to take your own maps and compass, just in case. If something really unexpected happens and you get separated from your leader or your group, you won't be clueless and helpless.

   A compass is also useful when you're wandering on your own during the "free time" that most companies schedule in cities and towns. Your leader or hotel probably will give you a map, but it might have the names of the main streets only. (Moreover, it might look like a labyrinth. You can't expect an easy-to-navigate Midwestern street grid in a third world town.) It's easy to get confused, but if you know your hotel is on the north side of town, you can at least get yourself headed in the right direction.

   Take both country or regional maps and city maps; enlarge them on a copying machine so you can read the street names (but don't expect to find marked streets in many developing countries). Rip the relevant pages from a couple of guidebooks and staple them together by country, region, and city. Keep this geography info together in a plastic Ziploc bag.

- **Flashlight.** A flashlight is a must on any trip. You never know when the power will fail and you'll be groping around an unfamiliar place in the dark. And on an adventure trip you could spend a lot of nights in places miles from any electricity.

   A small flashlight that packs a lot of power in a two-ounce cylinder will fit in your shirt pocket. A slightly larger model is said to be six times brighter than a regular flashlight, able to penetrate fog (and smoke if you're in a hotel fire). A headband light is good when you're camping: It frees your hands so you can carry things or hold a book when you're tucked into your sleeping bag.

   Whatever model you choose, be sure to take an extra bulb and a spare set of fresh batteries. (That's in addition to the fresh ones you should put in your flashlight before you go, especially if you'll be spending a lot of time in a tent.)
- **First-aid kit.** Don't depend on the leader's first-aid kit. Bring your own. (See Chapter 5 for details.)
- **Whistle.** If you're in trouble in town, a whistle will attract attention; if you're lost in the bush, it will direct rescuers. A series of three short blasts is the universal call for help. Instead of a child's plastic model get a high-decibel storm whistle that functions when wet.
- **Survival sack.** A popsicle-sized three-ounce survival sack provides emergency warmth insurance. Sometimes called space blankets, these are blaze orange on one side (for visibility in case you're lost or injured) and polyester/ mylar laminate on the inside to retain your body heat.

> **TIP**
>
> If you've never used a compass, practice at home with a map so you'll have some idea of how to orient yourself.

PERSONAL TRAVEL ITEMS

- **Notebook.** Carry a spiral notebook that fits into one of your cargo pockets, or get a bound blank journal at a bookstore (prettier but heavier). And take new ball-point pens—several, because you'll lose some along the way.

   A notebook will have all sorts of uses, not the least of which is to record your travel experiences. You also might want to take notes from time to time, such as the leader's instructions as to where and when to meet or how to find a recommended place to eat when it's a "dinner on your own" night. And it's always good to have blank paper for those interactions when you don't know the language—a map back to your hotel when you're lost, pages for drawings by and for children, a place for a shopkeeper to write down a price for you so you'll understand the answer to your question, "How much?"

- **Calculator.** A pocket calculator is invaluable for doing dollar conversions. Fancy models have a language dictionary. The third world language you'll need probably won't be available, but if your model has a micro word processor, you can enter your own personal vocabulary list.

- **Vocabulary list.** A pocket dictionary is handy, though it might be hard to find one in the language you need. Even if you do have a dictionary, you'll find that bringing a list of basic words on a couple of three-by-five cards—or on your minicomputer—will make communicating in a hurry much easier. Don't clutter your cards (or your mind) with verbs and prepositions. You might want to include a few key adjectives and adverbs, but your list should consist mainly of nouns. They're all you'll really need to get by.

  When compiling your vocabulary list, start with the polite basics: *hello, good-bye, please, thank you, excuse me.* If you're going to be taking photos, add *okay?* for those times when you want to take close-ups of people. Then add some of the words in most guidebooks' foreign-language sections: *how much, yes, no,* and some food words. *Pretty* followed by *baby* or *child* is a wonderful icebreaker that always earns you a smile.

  Then add some emergency words. You'll need to recognize key words written on signs, such as *exit, stop,* and *danger.* Think about your itinerary. Are you going on a ferry? If so it will be good to be able to recognize words such as *life jacket* and *lifeboat* so you can scope out their locations.

- **Kwikpoint.** A Kwikpoint is nice to have when words fail. These little folders are filled with miniature drawings of hundreds of objects, with everything from toilet to taxi. Just point to what you need and say *help, please.*

PERSONAL HYGIENE

- **Cleansers.** A little plastic bottle of all-purpose biodegradable liquid soap will do it all: hair, skin, and socks. Dr. Bronners is an old backpackers' standby (and if you've finished reading everything you and everyone else brought, the label is mildly entertaining). You can also take soap wafers—a hundred in a Ziploc weigh less than half an ounce.

  For those times when you're covered with dust with no wash water handy, you can still freshen up. Put a few antibiotic moist wipes in a plastic Ziploc in your daypack so you can clean your hands before you eat. There's also a liquid antibiotic "instant hand sanitizer" said to kill "99.9% of germs." You put a small amount in your palm and rub your hands together briskly until they're dry.

  For nights in primitive camps, you can get some of that just-showered feeling with dry shampoos and cleansers designed for no-rinse situations, or you can use a high-end wipe with built-in, no-rinse cleanser plus moisturizer. A packet of eight weighs four ounces.

- **Washcloths.** These small cloths are scarce even in European hotels, so don't expect to find them in adventure travel locations. But you don't want to take your own and deal with constantly damp terry cloth. Get a package of Handi-wipes—thin, tough, synthetic cloths found in the cleaning products aisle of the grocery store. Cut some in half and use them as washcloths. They dry in minutes and fold up into tiny squares. (They're designed as disposables but will last through any two- or three-week trip.)

- **Tooth care items.** For tooth care, think small. A travel-size tube of toothpaste will last a long time. (Test one at home to see if it'll get you through two or three weeks.) Get a camping toothbrush—half the length of a normal one—that comes with a plastic cover. Keep the

> **TIP**
>
> Many guidebooks have entire sentences (such as *Where is the toilet?*) in their vocabulary sections. But if you ask a question in a complete sentence, locals will often assume you're somewhat proficient in their language and respond in an incomprehensible torrent of words. Just *toilet?* with an inquiring look and tone is much more effective: You've conveyed what you need to know plus the fact that you need gestures or a map drawn on paper.

> **TIP**
>
> When you create your vocabulary list, put the phonetic pronunciation next to each word.

TIP

Some travel companies will tell you to bring a bath towel. If you don't want this sort of bulk in your bag, you can use your quick-drying fleece top, but a Paktowel is the best solution. This quick-dry miracle fabric absorbs about ten times its weight in moisture. A square about two feet by one foot weighs less than two ounces, but that's enough to do the job of a regular-size bath towel.

TIP

Keep the plastic cover on your toothbrush at night. A common—and particularly loathsome—insect likes the flavor of toothpaste.

FOR WOMEN ONLY

Take an adequate supply of tampons and pads, and take extra Ziplocs so you can wait until you get to a place where you can properly dispose of used ones. Take some minipads if you'll be trekking far from toilets. They help you minimize toilet paper use when you stop to pee, and they make the whole operation faster.

toothpaste in a Ziploc just in case the tube gets punctured. As for dental floss, take the right number of precut strands.

- **Personal items.** Tissues, comb, razor (not disposable), antiperspirant (no fragrance), safe sex/birth control supplies, cotton-tipped swabs, toenail clippers or tiny scissors, and footcare products; also, insect repellent, netting, sunscreen, and lip balm (see Chapter 5).

- **Moisturizer.** Be sure to bring a moisturizer—a tube or plastic jar of cream, not a lotion that's mostly liquid. Unless you're in a jungle, your skin is likely to feel parched. High altitudes, desert conditions, and airline cabins are major skin dehydrators.

THE EYES HAVE IT

Far from home and an optometrist, you need to take good care of your eyes.

- **Sunglasses.** If you'll be spending much time on snow or ice, choose a wraparound style or glacier glasses (with leather side shields and bridge cover). Make sure you get lenses with 100 percent UV protection.

- **Crushproof eyeglass case.** (These come in wraparound size, too.)

- **Extras.** Spare contacts or prescription glasses don't take up much room but could prove invaluable.

- **Chums** or **Croakies.** Those knit tubes that fit around the ear pieces of your glasses and go around the back of your head can keep you from losing your glasses. Especially good for paddling, they're great anywhere to ensure against leaving your sunglasses sitting on a table or rock somewhere.

- **Repair kit.** One of those tiny little plastic cases with a miniature screwdriver and eyeglass screws could come in handy.

- **Moisturizing drops.** You might need these to combat eyestrain from dry air and bright sun.

MISCELLANEOUS

- **Binoculars.** These are a must if you're going on a trip to spot birds or animals. They come in pocket-sized, ultralight models.
- **Umbrella.** Many travelers like these for trips to countries with intense sun or tropical downpours. You can get a "windproof" one that's less than a foot long and less than three-quarters of a pound.
- **Alarm.** You don't want to wake up some morning and find you've missed breakfast and barely have time to meet your van. Get an inexpensive but rugged watch/alarm combination, water resistant, with a night light.
- **Luggage lock.** Secure your zipper pulls with a four-ounce combination model that lets you change the numbers.
- **Bandanna.** This scarf can do a lot more than provide a flash of color at your neckline. You can pull it up over your nose if the dust gets thick on an open-vehicle trip; with a collarless shirt you can use it to prevent back-of-the-neck sunburn and chafing from camera or binocular straps; or you can use it as a head covering, emergency bandage, or handkerchief.
- **Comfort items.** Take saline nose spray in case of dry air or clogged sinuses; cough drops for a dry throat or hacking cough; hard candy for your sweet tooth.
- **Reading material.** Take a paperback book. You probably can trade with fellow travelers when you're finished.

> **TIP**
>
> If you don't mind spending more for a watch, there are some great features you can get in addition to timekeeping: thermometer, barometer, digital compass, altimeter, twenty-four-hour time. (Although with a leader you shouldn't need to know how high you've climbed, it's nice to have an altimeter function—if there is some question about where you are, an altimeter can help pinpoint your location.)
>
> **TIP**
>
> Get a bandanna with first-aid and survival instructions printed on it.

FIX-IT ITEMS

- **Personal repair kit.** Assemble a mini repair kit, including medium and large safety pins, extra dental floss and a large-eyed needle (so you can stitch tough fabrics back together), and a strip of duct tape rolled around your flashlight or trekking pole.
- **Swiss Army knife.** This will be the only tool you'll need (unless you're bicycling). With this "pocket survival tool" you can cut, slice, dice, file, tweeze, open a soup can, and flip a beer cap, just for starters. Fancier models offer a wider variety of tools, including a ruler,

screwdriver, pliers, saw, and corkscrew. (But be careful: Those gadgets can make your pack weight creep up. A stripped-down model weighs only two ounces, while the deluxe version weighs nine ounces. Since you want a basic utility and emergency tool, go with the lightweight version—or the newer "Swiss card," which features ten implements in a one-ounce, credit-card–sized kit.)

WATER

On an active trip you'll get thirsty and, more importantly, your body will need more fluid than you might think to keep you safely hydrated. During the day you'll carry your own water, and you have some container options.

- **Containers.** Lexan (a high-impact plastic) pint- and quart-size water bottles with wide-mouth screw tops are today's improved version of the old Boy Scout canteen. Depending on conditions, you could need as much as a gallon between the resupplying provided by your trip leader, so make sure you have enough bottles. An alternative to the standard bottle is a soft water bottle that collapses as you drink. A real space-saver, it rolls up like a toothpaste tube as you empty it.

  You'll be buying a lot of bottled water—whenever you stop in a village with safe supplies for sale. For ease in carrying these bottles around, you can get a sling called a waterporter. Worn like a shoulder bag, it holds 1- and 1.5-liter plastic water bottles.

- **Purifiers.** Adventure companies normally supply safe drinking water, but it's prudent to have a backup such as iodine pills (see page 70). Or get one of the new soda can–sized water filters. Look for one with both a micro-filter and an iodine matrix, a combination that will eliminate protozoa and kill bacteria and viruses.

MUSCLE FUELS

Even though your adventure company will supply virtually all your food, there will be times when you'll be happy you have your own minilarder.

- **Energy bars.** When you start dragging, you'll want a snack. But the snacks that give you a quick boost will send your blood sugar through the roof. After that early spike your blood sugar level will plummet, and you'll feel weaker than before. Carry some of the energy bars sold in outdoors stores. Often called "performance food," these bars come in a variety of flavors from wild berry to espresso. They pack a lot of punch in a little package— a lot more than the cereal bars on your grocery shelf.

If you're health conscious you've probably cut back on the fat in your diet (and the protein as well) and have opted for a preponderance of complex carbohydrates. But on a trip you might want to temporarily boost your fat and protein intake: Protein and fat metabolize more slowly than carbohydrates and give you a steady fuel supply for a longer period of time. Some food bars will give you almost equal portions of carbo, fat, and protein. Having a snack like this in your pocket might enable you to hike or paddle those last few miles.

> **TIP**
>
> Take some M&Ms in Ziplocs to assuage your chocolate cravings when you're far from a candy counter.

THE FOLKS BACK HOME

- **Phone service.** Chances are you won't need to phone home, but in case you have to call it'll help if you've written down the overseas number to use with your particular long-distance service.
- **Address labels.** For sending those "you'll never believe what we just saw" reports of leopards or llamas, take preaddressed labels instead of your address book.

MAKING NEW FRIENDS

One of the joys of adventure travel is meeting people of different cultures in remote regions relatively untouched by civilization. Planning for your encounters can enrich your interactions.

- **Toys and gifts.** Curious children often are attracted to adventure travel camps. Take a Koosh (one of those soft and fluffy little balls that looks like a sea urchin). It weighs next to nothing in your bag, and it's an easy and gentle way to play catch. A kazoo or harmonica is a great musical icebreaker for all ages. Be prepared in case you're invited into a home: Bring useful, non-plastic gifts such as maps, pencils, color postcards. (For more on gift-giving, see page 142.)
- **Tape recorder.** With a tape recorder, you can bring home the sounds to go with the sights your camera cap-

tures—tribal songs, howler monkeys, screeching parrots. A five-inch-long model will fit in one of your cargo pockets.

CAPTURING THE SIGHTS

- **Camera and filters.** Choosing a camera involves a lot of tradeoffs. A point-and-shoot camera provides quick and easy shots and weighs twelve ounces. With some newer pocket-size models you get spot metering, focus lock, a zoom lens, and a variety of shooting options, such as fill flash and panoramic mode. But if you're a serious photographer you might feel it's worth the extra space and weight to bring a camera with faster lenses, telephoto capability, and special filters. (Most filters are optional, but one is a must: a haze, UV skylight, or neutral-density filter to protect the lens.)

- **Tripod.** Photographers often use tripods to capture low-light scenes and to allow them to use long exposures to increase depth of field. Normal tripods are too heavy and bulky for many adventure trips, but there are miniatures that are reasonable substitutes. Ultralight models weigh only a few ounces and have numerous stabilizing options.

- **Camera bag.** Put your camera in a Ziploc bag. Dust often is a problem in some adventure travel regions. It can coat your equipment with a fine layer and even freeze the shutter action. And if you're headed for the humid jungle, take a desiccant.

- **Film.** Be sure to take enough film. In developing countries, film supplies are often nonexistent, wildly expensive, or out of date. According to an old rule for packing for a vacation, after you've selected your clothing you should leave half of it at home. With film, it's the opposite: You'll never have too many rolls! Here's a basic guideline: If you're shooting thirty-six–exposure film, pack one roll for every day you'll be adventuring. Professionals often say they're happy if they get one "keeper" out of three dozen slides, so the more film you take, the better your chances. Besides, you'll be surprised at how many times you'll pull your camera out to capture another stunning memory.

- **Batteries and lens cleaner.** Pick up spare camera batteries when you buy your trip film. If your batteries fail in the outback you'll be out of luck. Even if you've recently replaced your batteries, get new ones and pack them in a little Ziploc along with a lens brush and some lens cloths and cleaner.

To save space and make things easier at airports, take your film out of those little cardboard boxes. Mark the top of each canister with the film's ASA and expiration date and put them in a see-through Ziploc.

Experts disagree as to the danger of film passing through airport X-ray machines. Most say film with speeds of 400 ASA or below won't be damaged. But a trip like this is unusual: You'll be going through more airports, and some foreign airport machines will zap your film with stronger doses. Also, depending on the trip, you might be shooting high-speed film (for East African big-game shots in the early morning and late afternoon, for example).

- **Film shield bag.** You can't always persuade guards to hand-inspect your film (even if you've removed the film boxes and have your film in a clear plastic bag). Bring a radiationproof film shield bag to protect your film from X-ray damage. Some bags are rather bulky, but the newer ones fold up, fasten with Velcro, and hold three dozen rolls.

TIP

If you don't have binoculars, your telephoto lens can function as a makeshift telescope.

TIP

If you're carrying more than about two dozen rolls of film, you might get pegged as a professional at some entry points, and officials might make you cough up high fees for permits. If you can, split your supply with a traveling companion.

TIP

Never put your film in a bag you'll be checking. Aside from the fact that you might never see it again, there's the chance it could get zapped with megadeath rays by a security scanner designed to detect explosives in checked baggage.

TIP

Some films come in clear canisters. If yours doesn't, ask your camera shop if you can rummage through their recycling bin and pick out some. Airport security workers are more likely to agree to hand-inspect your film if they don't have to pry the lids off all those little canisters.

IN MOTION

GET OUT A GLOBE AND LOCATE WHERE YOU WANT TO GO. It's a long way down to Peru or Patagonia. And if you're bound for a spot halfway around the world, you'll spend even more grueling hours in the air on multiple flights that could add up to a forty-eight-hour marathon.

Some frequent time-zone changers say jet-lag diets help. But you might be too busy with last-minute details to worry about special foods and a new schedule. There are items that will help, however, once you're in flight.

- **In-flight items.** You can ease the transition if you sleep or even just rest with your eyes closed when it's nighttime in your destination time zone. Bring an eye mask—one of those block-the-light models—and ear plugs. If you're susceptible to ear pain on landings bring a nasal decongestant spray and some EarPlanes (devices with porous ceramic filters that slow the rate of air-pressure changes in the ear canal).

- **Motion sickness aids.** Once you begin your real adventure traveling, you might encounter other problems. For any sort of watery passage it's a good idea to have some weapons to combat motion sickness: Dramamine, behind-the-ear patches, motion bands for your wrists. Even if your trip is completely on dry land, you could still suffer from motion sickness on endless, rocky, curvy roads switchbacking up and down mountain passes.

FOR WOMEN ONLY

If you're on birth-control pills or hormone-replacement therapy, you could have an added risk for blood clotting in your legs on long flights. You can get special travel socks—similar to those used in hospitals—that will improve your circulation.

TREKKING EQUIPMENT

- **Trekking pole.** If you've always walked on smooth paths, you might wonder why you'd need a steadying tool. But it's great to have something to lean on when you're on slippery moss or wobbly rocks or hopping from stone to stone crossing a stream. A trekking pole is like a helping hand. Made of lightweight aluminum, it has three sections so you can adjust it according to the terrain—shorter going uphill and longer on the downhill.

- **Gaiters.** Gaiters are like little raincoats for your ankles and shins. They're made of tough nylon with a heel strap to hold them on. They'll keep your pants dry when you're wading through tall wet grasses or mountain snowfields, and they'll keep water or snow from sneaking into your socks via your boot tops.

- **Bag liner.** Adventure companies often supply sleeping bags for camping treks, but it's nice to have something between you and that rental bag. A silk sleeping-bag liner weighs less than six ounces and stuffs into a tiny bag. (Even if you're not camping, a liner is handy when you're confronted with questionable sheets.)

- **Sleeping bag.** If you need to bring your own bag and you don't have one, remember when you're buying or borrowing that superlight goose down provides warm and fluffy insulation only when it's dry. And after it gets wet, a down bag dries much more slowly than a synthetic one.

  You'll also need to consider temperature ratings. Your adventure company should be able to tell you the expected overnight lows at your various altitudes. When you're shopping for a bag you'll see ratings from −20° to +30° Fahrenheit. Since you can always pull on more layers if you're cold or open up the zipper if you're hot, you have a lot of leeway, but you do want to make sure you won't be shivering after you've pulled on everything in your pack.

- **Pad.** Make sure the travel company will provide something to put between you and the ground. Many do, but if you're supposed to supply your own sleeping equipment, a pad is essential. Open-cell foam with a nylon cover, such as Therm-a-Rest, provides insulation and padding—enough for a surprisingly comfortable night's sleep.

- **Chair conversion kit.** After several days, campers often long for something to sit on that has a back they can lean against. If yours is a "soft" adventure you'll probably have chairs and tables in camp. But if you'll be expected to sit on little stools or cross-legged on the ground, you might want to take a ten-ounce chair-rest kit that will turn your sleeping pad into a camp chair.

- **Extra duffel.** Trekkers take their duffels and daypacks with them, but there usually are a few items—such as souvenirs and city clothes—that they want to leave behind at the hotel. Take a small nylon bag with a zipper for your nonessentials.

> **TIP**
>
> There might be times when you won't want to leave your tent, no matter how urgently nature is calling. You might get a warning in lion country to "stay within three feet of your tent during the night," or you could be high in the mountains and hate the idea of going out in the cold. For men, an extra Lexan bottle can serve as a pee pot; women can get a palm-size "portable restroom" device from a camping-supply specialist.

> **TIP**
>
> Sleeping bag temperature ratings aren't as precise as your home's thermostat. If you're the one who reaches for a sweater when others are still in short sleeves, get a bag with a lower temperature rating.

ADVENTURE SPORTS GEAR

ADVENTURE TRIPS USUALLY INVOLVE SOME WALKING, BUT when your main activity is something more—cycling, paddling, horseback riding—you'll need specialized gear. Follow your company's packing list carefully.

- **Helmet.** All three of those sports have a risk of head injury. Bicyclists call their helmets "brain buckets" and know that these head huggers can save them from serious injury or even death from a fall not just on asphalt, but even on dirt. The same is true for paddlers in major rapids or equestrians on galloping horses. Make sure your company will provide safe helmets. If not, bring your own.

- **Cycling accessories.** Bicycling is a popular way to move through the countryside in exotic regions. Companies usually provide the bicycles, but there are other items you'll need. You won't be able to wear a broad-brimmed sun hat, so bring a visor to protect your face. Most cyclists wear padded cycling shorts and padded gloves. You might want biking shoes (check to see if you'll need the kind that clip on to the pedals—your travel company should be able to tell you what kind of pedals/clips are on the bikes and if you need special shoes to match). If even part of your trip will be on roads, consider some safety items as well: a reflective vest in case a day's ride unexpectedly ends after dark, and a tiny cyclist's mirror that attaches to your helmet and lets you check on traffic approaching from behind.

  You can use your rain gear as a windbreaker if it's made of breathable fabric. Under your helmet you can wear a neoprene ear band or a thin balaclava. And for comfort you might want to bring your own gel-cushioned saddle pad, depending on how many daily hours in the saddle you'll have.

- **Paddling items.** On the water, you might need a sun visor, extra tubes of waterproof sunscreen, water sandals, waterproof gear bag, inflatable/watertight camera pouch, water-sports wallet, and neoprene top, bottom, boots, or gloves. (If the trip involves major rapids, make sure the company provides helmets.)

  Like a helmet for cycling, a life vest is a crucial piece of safety equipment for paddling and rafting. An outfitter might have those old-style kapok life jackets, which might have outlived their ability to hold a person up in the water. If there's any question about what your company will supply, you can take your own modern personal flotation device (PFD)—a front-zip nylon model with foam flotation sewn in vertical tubes. And don't forget something to hold your glasses on your face: If they fall off in the water, they're gone!

- **Equestrian items.** Horseback riders will need special items as well, such as boots and a hard hat. Follow your outfitter's checklist, and if you're a neophyte equestrian, ask people at a nearby stable for their advice.

> ### FOR WOMEN ONLY
>
> A specially designed bicycle seat for females is shaped to protect sensitive anatomy. Check with your company to see if you'd be able to switch the seat on its bike.
>
> ### TIP
>
> For trips that include extensive snorkeling, it might be worth the extra weight and space to take your own mask. It's often hard to find one that seals well among those provided at the destination.

PACKING IT IN

BY NOW YOU'RE PROBABLY THINKING YOU'LL NEED A steamer trunk for all this gear. Not so! If you choose carefully, just about all of your clothing and equipment will be small enough to fit in a duffel and a daypack. Your hiking boots might be the exception, but you can carry them by wearing them on the plane. (After you arrive at your destination you can tie them onto your duffel strap when you're not using them.)

As for your "luggage," grungy is better than Gucci. Go for the scuffed, student look, not a new, upscale style. If the outside doesn't look valuable, the better the chances that a thief won't go looking for valuables inside. (That rules out leather, which looks much too good, and is much too heavy as well.) A nondescript bag won't announce, "I'm an American tourist, ripe for the plucking."

You'll need three basic containers: a travel wallet, a large pack or duffel, and a daypack.

YOUR TRAVEL WALLET: A (HIDDEN) ASSET

Far from home, it's best to play it safe where your valuables are concerned. You'll want to make sure you have the essentials—such as your tickets, passport, and credit cards—with you at all times, and you'll want to keep them in something that's tough, lightweight, and easy to keep out of sight.

So your regular wallet and handbag stay at home. Travel gear manufacturers have come up with alternatives that are much better security bets. Both are made of lightweight nylon, with adjustable cords or straps and three or more separate compartments. Best of all, they're inconspicuous. A neck pouch is suspended on a cord and can be worn out of sight beneath your shirt (down in front or at the side). A security belt is worn around your waist, usually under your shirt just above your waistband.

If you're wearing a loose, oversized shirt, either of these security wallets will be virtually invisible. Both are worn on the front of your body, impervious to the sort of sneak attacks that occur with vulnerable shoulder bags and pocket wallets. And if it's even slightly noticeable, it'll just look like you've put on a little bit of weight around the middle. (Remember, on this kind of a trip, you're better off dressing for function, not for looks!)

TIP

In hot climates you'll be wearing your security wallet next to your skin. Look for one with a soft nylon backing that feels like cotton.

Travel Wallet Essentials: You probably could get by with the clothes on your back, as long as you had your money and your travel documents. Here are the absolute essentials to stash in your travel wallet:

- **Passport** with an expiration date that's six months after your return date.
- **Visas** for stopover countries as well as for destinations. Your travel company should tell you which countries require visas and how to get them. You can get visas directly from embassies or consulates, but it often saves time and trouble to pay a visa service to get what you need.
- **International Certificate of Vaccination.** The official yellow card with the doctor-signed record of your immunizations and your personal medical history. Staple this to the back inside cover of your passport. Use a stick-on label for your medical- and travel-insurance information: name of the company, phone number, and your policy number.
- **Airline tickets.**
- **Adventure travel company vouchers.** Your receipts for your payment in full, the admission tickets you'll present to your trip leader, and perhaps for your hotel when you arrive at the starting point.
- **Some American money.** Dollar bills—and maybe some fives as well. These are accepted in a surprising number of places and will come in handy as tips or emergency cash when you haven't converted traveler's checks

or when you've run out of local currency.

- **Credit cards.** Tape a little label on each card with the company's overseas travel assistance number.
- **Traveler's checks.**
- **Travel/medical insurance card.**
- **Flight schedule** plus instructions for finding your group when you get to Timbuktu or Kathmandu.

> **TIP**
>
> Most people like to take along a copy of their day-by-day itinerary, either in their travel wallet or in a pocket of their daypack.

Don't Put All Your Eggs in One Basket: Now you're ready for anything—unless you lose your travel wallet! But even if the worst happens, you won't despair if you've made copies—in quadruplicate.

- **Photocopies.** Make four copies of:
  - the identification page of your passport
  - visas
  - traveler's check numbers
  - credit cards
  - airline tickets
  - adventure travel company vouchers
  - flight numbers and directions
  - phone numbers of IAMAT doctors (see Chapter 5)
  - phone numbers of U.S. embassy and consulates
  - emergency credit card phone numbers

> **TIP**
>
> Along with copies of the essential papers, leave a copy of your day-by-day itinerary at home along with the phone number of the U.S. office of your adventure travel company. Some companies operate field offices; if there's one in your destination country, get that number also. All of this will help speed contact with you in case of an emergency back home.

Some travel experts say it's a good idea to make copies of your birth certificate to expedite passport replacement if necessary. Also make photocopies of prescriptions, any letters from your physician, and your official immunization record, including the section on your medical history. (See Chapter 5.)

Leave two sets of copies with a friend or family member back home, tuck another in your clothes bag, and give the third set to your traveling companion. Nothing's fail-safe, but this backup system is about as close as you can get to covering all the bases.

YOUR DUFFEL

Experienced travelers will tell you, "There are two kinds of luggage: carry-on and lost."

The best duffel is big enough to carry what you (really) need, yet small enough to carry on the plane with you. Check your airline's specifications for carry-on size. On most international flights you should be able to get a three-week duffel into the overhead compartment. Not only will you avoid delays, your crucial gear will arrive when you do.

Experienced adventure travelers also know that their pack or duffel had better be the "right stuff." It's worth it to pay for quality. You'll need something that's much tougher than the lightweight nylon bag you'd take on a city getaway. If you become an adventure traveler, this bag will lead an exciting life—left in tropical downpours, stuffed on roof racks, dumped in dirt, slung on yaks. So, look for these features:

- Rugged, rip- and abrasionproof nylon with a waterproof coating on the inside (such as Cordura Plus)
- Quality construction (reinforced stress points, durable hardware, taped seams, sturdy buckles, industrial lock stitching that won't unravel)
- Industrial-strength zippers (double-stitched, nylon coil), the kind that repair themselves if the slider runs off the track

Convertibles: Some duffels are convertible backpacks in disguise. They have a hidden shoulder strap system so you can switch from carry-on to backpack—a good combination for those times when you have to lug your bag long distances or up and down stairs. And some convertibles have more options: wheels and a pull-out handle so you can pull your bag along behind you.

Bag It: Your duffel or backpack might be water resistant, but get some waterproof, coated-nylon stuff sacks for your clothes. These help with organizing as well—tops in one, pants in another, a bag with cold-weather items, and so on.

Group smaller items in clear freezer-type Ziplocs. They'll keep dust and water out and you'll be able to find what you need in a hurry instead of rummaging through a big bag of jumbled-up items. Include a Ziploc filled with extra freezer bags—gallon to pint size.

Slip in a few plastic garbage bags as well. You can sit on them when it's damp or dirty. And if you're caught without your rain gear, cut holes for your arms and head and use one as an emergency poncho.

YOUR DAYPACK

When you're hiking or cycling, you'll be free of your heaviest burden—the duffel. But even with yaks, porters, or vehicle support, you'll still have to carry whatever you'll need during the day, such as water, extra layers, and camera gear.

Look for a daypack made of that same rugged and weatherproof nylon as your duffel. Zippered pockets on the outside will come in handy for such items as a water bottle and telephoto lens.

Even if you're only carrying a day's worth of essentials on your back, you'll be surprised at how the weight adds up. So look for a daypack that has padded shoulder straps that cushion the load and distribute the weight. A hip belt will make a big difference in your day-after-day comfort, especially if you're carrying a lot of water and extra camera equipment. These padded belts transfer much of the weight to your hips— you'll be much more comfortable if your shoulders aren't carrying the whole load, and you'll tire less quickly, too.

Some convertible packs have a main duffel/pack with a detachable daypack, and some even have a three-in-one bonus, with both a detachable daypack and a removable waist pack. There's only one downside to this: You might not get a padded hip belt or several outside pockets on your daypack if you opt for this combo.

ROOM FOR EXPANSION

You should plan now for your return trip. When you're ready to head home from the exotic world you've been exploring, you'll probably have more than you came with, such as those carvings you bought at the village market.

TIP

Camping-equipment stores sell "compression sacks" for bulky sleeping bags. Backpackers use these so they'll have more room in their backpacks for the rest of their gear, but you can use the same technique with your clothes. Cinch those straps and you'll compress the contents to about half their original bulk. You might have a few more wrinkles, but this is an adventure travel trip—looks don't count.

FOR WOMEN ONLY

If your shoulder straps tend to slip off, buy a sternum strap from a camping outfitter. This little adjustable strap goes across your chest just below your collarbone and connects your two shoulder straps, pulling them toward each other and keeping them from slipping off.

You can solve this no-space-for-souvenirs problem in advance if you buy an expandable-style bag that "grows" when you need more space. These bags start out at carry-on size, with dimensions that conform to standard under-the-seat or over-head-bin specifications. (Your souvenir-filled bag will probably be too bulky for the overhead bin, but on your return flights you can check it because you won't be so worried about landing without your gear.)

Here's another alternative: Check your duffel and carry on that lightweight nylon bag you brought along for just this reason.

CHAPTER 8

STAYING SAFE

L IKE SCHOOL CHILDREN ON A FIELD TRIP, MANY ADVEN-
ture travelers move along without a care in the world, as if
they're enclosed in a protective bubble. They glide
through their itineraries, feeling immune from danger with their
American flock. Most of these travelers *are* quite safe, with every
reason to blithely enjoy their trip of a lifetime. However, there are
exceptions—from mere annoyances to real threats. And the smart
traveler goes forth to a strange new world—one with big gaps in its
safety net—aware of what could happen and prepared to deal with
unpleasant surprises.

Crime is an increasing problem in many developing countries,
ranging from snatch-and-grab to armed robbery. In more extreme
cases, there's kidnapping, extortion, and the shooting of those who
try to resist. Disasters can happen anywhere at any time—hotels

burn, ferries sink, the earth quakes. Moreover, there are some very unstable countries among prime adventure travel destinations, so there's a greater chance of running into riots, insurgencies, and terrorists. At times, traveling with a group can make you more of a target for terrorist attacks.

There are a few things you can do before you go to prepare for such emergencies. Certain items tucked in your pack—and certain info filed in your brain—could help you get out of trouble and back to safety.

PREVENTING THEFTS

THE STATE DEPARTMENT'S CONSULAR INFORMATION SHEETS note the degree of criminal activity in a country's major cities. Check for a description of the city where you'll be landing to meet your group. If some degree of caution is indicated, find out while you're still in the States how you should cope if for some reason you're not met by a company representative at the airport. Find out how to get to your hotel. Know in advance if you should avoid taxis, or just some kinds of taxis. If you're taking a bus, know where to find it and how to identify the right one. And always remember that in many countries, thieves frequent airports and bus stations, looking for unwary travelers.

Scruffy vagabond students usually have less trouble with thefts and robberies. If you're too old to achieve that look, go for the aging-hippie image. Just as with luggage, the worn-and-battered look is best for clothing.

Here are some other ways to improve your chances of keeping your possessions:

- Sew a wire into the strap of your neck pouch so a thief can't cut or yank it away. You can also look for this feature in a new pouch.
- Travel light. The less you're carrying, the faster you'll be able to move if you encounter problems on a train platform or street corner. And with a light bag (backpack or shoulder duffel) you won't be tempted to take it off for a minute and set it down—where it might get snatched.
- Use the luggage tags with flaps that obscure your name and home country.
- On the luggage tags, use something other than your home address. Use your business phone number and the phone

number of a friend or family member back home who knows your itinerary. That way, if your luggage goes astray the airline won't be calling your empty house—and no untrustworthy types will know your house is empty.

- Use a thick, permanent magic marker or black electrical tape to cover the logos on your bags, camera, and shoes.
- Pack clothing without logos or slogans that would instantly label you as an American.
- Leave your "I'm a tourist" camera bag at home. Take clothing—shirt, pants, vest, jacket—with lots of handy pockets instead.

> **TIP**
>
> Don't skimp on the quality of your hiking boots if you're going to be doing much walking. But if you're taking an extra pair of shoes, such as running shoes, take a rundown, off-brand, cheap pair. If your clothing is nondescript a potential thief might size you up by the look of your shoes. If you're not a walking specimen of American affluence you won't look like such a good prospect.

> **TIP**
>
> Learn how to say *no money*. A shrug with this phrase, coupled with a slightly shabby outfit, works very well in situations where you're surrounded by people who want to sell you something.

COPING WITH DISASTERS

PREPARE AN EMERGENCY CARD WITH SOME key words and phrases—with phonetic pronunciations—written both in English and the language (and alphabet) of your destination country. You need to be able to recognize crucial warnings either when you see them or hear them. Some helpful words and phrases to be able to use and understand in a crisis include *fire, help, danger, police, doctor, ambulance, come here, get out, turn around, flood, emergency brake, emergency exit, lifeboat, life jacket.*

For any emergency or disruption—civil, natural, or criminal—you'll have a far better chance of coping if you've figured out ahead of time how to react.

In many third world countries, the crowds on transportation systems exceed safe capacity. The "official" number allowed often bears no resemblance to the massive hordes that push on board, especially during holidays. If you find yourself on a dangerously overcrowded conveyance, check out the location of emergency exits or lifeboats and life jackets and hang out in the vicinity—just in case.

Hotels without sprinkler systems or proper fire escapes are common in third world countries. In case of fire:

- Stay close to the floor.
- Fill your bathtub and sink with water.

- Seal vents and cracks around doors with duct tape (you wrapped some around your hiking stick or flashlight, remember?).
- Hang something white, like a sheet, outside the window so rescuers will know where you are.

The terra isn't always firma in many adventure travel spots. In seismically unstable regions, if the earth starts to move under your feet you'll be glad if you know whether you're supposed to jump in the bathtub or run outside. (Hint: Tubs are for tornadoes.)

In the event of a temblor, head outside *only* if you can do so very quickly and if going outdoors will not place you in danger of being struck by debris falling from nearby buildings. Otherwise, get under a door frame, a desk, or other solid structure, cover your head, and wait it out. Once the initial shaking stops, get outside and into the open immediately.

> **TIP**
>
> Knowing the word for *fire* can be doubly useful, in case of flames and in case of attack or robbery. In some instances, you might be able to attract more attention if you yell *fire* instead of *help* or *police*.

IF YOU'RE IN THE RIGHT PLACE AT THE WRONG TIME

MANY ADVENTURE TRAVELERS TEND TO BE FAR TOO RELIANT on their leader, secure on an imaginary tether to their protector. But have you ever been in a small plane at 5,000 feet and wondered what you would do if the pilot passed out? Ever been aboard a sailboat on the ocean and wondered what you would do if the skipper fell overboard?

Think about preparing yourself to be self-reliant in case something happens to your leader far from any backup. Despite a company's experience and prudence, there's a remote but real possibility you could find yourself in the middle of something that surprises even the security experts. Depending on where you are at the time, you might get separated from your trip leader, in which case it would be nice to have some idea of what to do and where to go next. Before you leave home:

- Get the number of the U.S. embassy's recorded security updates.
- Obtain maps of the major cities you'll be visiting.

> **TIP**
>
> In the case of a serious disturbance, if you have enough time buy a supply of nonperishable food—cookies, crackers, whatever will keep—plus as much bottled water as you can carry. Get back to your hotel and stay there. Pull the drapes and put your blanket and bedspread over the curtain rod. Take down any mirrors and fill your bathtub. Then keep your head down, below window level.

- Mark the routes to the U.S. embassy and consulates.
- Know what to do in case there's rioting or gunfire.

TRIP EXTENSIONS

SINCE YOU'RE ALREADY TRAVELING SO FAR, YOU MIGHT decide to see a bit more of the region after your regular adventure trip ends. So why not see another island or another city, and let the company make the arrangements for you? After all, its staff members are the experts on that country, aren't they? Maybe.

But maybe the company has the adventure trip area well covered—good intelligence on everything from the right subcontractors to the best lodgings—but isn't well informed about traveling outside that area. Maybe it's not up to date on guerrilla groups or bandits operating in the region where it's sending you.

For your primary trip your company might be quite particular about how it gets you from the city where you land to the frontier and back again, finding the most reliable drivers, vehicles, or airplanes, and if you ask for additional arrangements outside its scope of operation, you might get an equal level of careful scrutiny and informed choices. Or it might just use the yellow pages approach to book your travel arrangements.

If you want an add-on trip, it's best to do the same research you did when choosing your original destination and company. Ask your outfit some questions before you book any extension:

- Have you sent any other clients on the same extension? May I have their names and numbers?
- How did you find this subcontractor?
- What do you know about the safety of the transportation?
- Is that region of the country stable? Are any guerrillas or bandits operating nearby?
- What about safety on the roads? Holdups? Dangerous conditions such as washouts?

IT HAPPENED

After a father and daughter finished their adventure travel trip, they journeyed to a jungle lodge for a few days of bird-watching. The adventure travel company had subcontracted this extension trip with the local outfit that operated the lodge. They were on one of the trails near the lodge when bandits jumped out of the jungle, robbed their fellow bird-watchers, and kidnapped the father. After five weeks he was rescued by the police—after a shoot-out in which four of the bandits were killed.

IT HAPPENED

A couple asked their adventure travel company to arrange an extension after their group trip. Their company booked them on a domestic "airline." The plane turned out to be an aging four-seater that took off in the rain with no visibility—and no instruments. The pilot grew more and more nervous, glancing right and left, peering through the murk, hoping for a break in the clouds. He dipped low and managed to find a landing strip instead of a mountaintop, but the couple opted to take a bus back.

Then check the latest State Department reports and other sources and look for any information related to your add-on region. (See the Appendix, page 159, for contact information at the State Department.)

CHAPTER 9

A PLANNING CALENDAR

ONE KEY TO A GREAT ADVENTURE IS AN EARLY START ON your trip planning. Give yourself plenty of time to choose wisely from the widest possible range of alternatives. And when you finalize your arrangements, leave enough time between sign-up and takeoff to prepare yourself for your big adventure. The following checklist outlines the basic steps to take—from the time the trip is just a gleam in your eye up through that last (not too hectic!) week before you get on the plane to your destination.

EIGHT MONTHS BEFORE DEPARTURE

❏ CHECK TRAVEL AND OUTDOORS MAGAZINES AND INTERNET sites for the names and numbers of adventure travel companies; call and ask for catalogs. (See Appendix, page 155, for a partial list.)

117

❏ When you receive the catalogs, choose trips that appeal to you and call the companies to request detailed itineraries.

❏ Check travel magazines and Internet sites for trip insurance ads. Call to request brochures. (See Appendix, page 157, for a partial list.)

❏ Go to your library and bookstore and research your dream destinations. Find out each country's best places to see what you're interested in: rare birds and wildlife; unique scenery; historical sites; fascinating cultures.

❏ Research the best times to visit your top choices: weather at the time you'll be traveling; dates of festivals; dates you might want to miss—such as contentious elections and anniversaries of uprisings.

❏ After you've selected your destination country, research the safety factors:

1. Assess the health risks—endemic diseases and available countermeasures (review Chapter 5).
2. Assess the transportation risks—the domestic carriers (review Chapter 4).
3. Assess the region's stability—the probability of bandits, terrorists, or insurgencies.

❏ Research your international airline alternatives, including prices and availability of flights.

❏ Call your adventure travel company candidates and ask for the names of people who have taken the particular trips you're interested in. Call these references. (See Chapter 3 for specific questions to ask them.)

❏ If you haven't had one recently, get a physical exam to make sure you don't have any serious underlying health problems or a condition that might prohibit intensified aerobic exercise.

❏ Call or meet with several travel agents and choose the one best suited to handle your adventure travel trip. Ask the agent to check on the adventure travel company; get feedback from adventure traveling clients; check on the availability of international flights for the dates you've chosen. (Flights to many adventure travel countries fill up much further in advance than flights to Europe.) (For more on working with a travel agent, see page 41.)

SIX MONTHS BEFORE DEPARTURE

THROUGHOUT THIS PERIOD, CONTINUE TO READ ABOUT YOUR destination. The more you know about its history and culture, the richer your experience will be.

❑ Finalize your five big decisions:
1. destination
2. adventure travel company
3. trip itinerary and date
4. international airline
5. trip insurance and medical insurance companies

❑ Have your travel agent make your trip and flight reservations.

❑ Lock in your trip insurance *the same day.*

❑ Check the date on your passport. Get it renewed if it will expire within six months of your return date. If you'll need visas, the passport should have one blank page left for each one you'll need.

❑ Get passport/visa photos, and order extras in case you lose your passport or unexpectedly need a visa en route.

❑ Get all necessary visas.

❑ Make an appointment at a travel clinic. Get advice on immunizations and preventive measures. Get travel medicine prescriptions, such as an antimalarial (see Chapter 5).

❑ See your family doctor. Make sure your health is "good to go" and that your childhood immunizations and boosters are up to date. Get prescriptions for emergency antibiotics. Discuss all your medications, including your travel clinic prescriptions, and find out about interactions and contraindications (see Chapter 5).

❑ Based on your medical history and doctors' recommendations, make a chart of what immunizations you'll need, how many shots in each series, and when you should get them. Begin getting immunizations. (Depending on your destination, it could take six months to complete your immunization schedule.)

❑ See your dentist. Schedule and complete all dental repairs.

❑ Join IAMAT and get their lists and publications (see page 159).

❑ Make an exercise schedule that includes both weight training and aerobic activities. Start your fitness program now—including your new office exercise regimen!

❑ Call travel product companies and outdoors companies and request their catalogs. (See Appendix, page 161, for partial list.) Start browsing at local outdoors sports and camping stores and travel equipment stores.

❑ Make a list of everything you'll need to take—from boots to batteries. Start purchasing clothing and gear.

❑ Buy your hiking boots now and start wearing them. Allow plenty of time to break them in—or to find out that those boots and your feet weren't meant to be together and you need to get another pair!

❑ Buy language tapes or dictionaries. Listen to the tapes as much as possible. Make a phonetic vocabulary list and start familiarizing yourself with the local lingo.

❑ If you plan on getting a new camera for your trip, buy it now and practice using it.

❑ Schedule weekend outings for the months ahead. You might need to go far afield to manage the best specificity training possible.

❑ Monitor your destination country's situation with respect to security risks, major weather anomalies, and emerging diseases (for more on monitoring these situations, see Chapters 2 and 5 and the Appendix).

❑ Check the tipping policies for your guide and staff. (To find details on this, call those references the company gave you and look through your pretrip info packet.) Check guidebooks for the country's practice for restaurants, too. (If 15 percent will be included automatically in your bill, you won't want to be dishing out more than 5 percent when you pay.)

❑ Make a list of all the things you need to do—from copying your records to clipping your toenails.

ONE MONTH BEFORE DEPARTURE

❑ GET YOUR PRESCRIPTIONS FILLED. (BY WAITING UNTIL now, you'll postpone those expiration dates.)

❑ Prepare your medical kit: medications, first-aid supplies, and instructions (see Chapter 5).

❑ Check your progress on your "to do" list.

❑ Make a vocabulary card that you'll always carry with you. Memorize the friendly greeting phrases—and the emergency ones. If you really need to yell *help*, you won't have time to look it up.

❏ Fresher is better. Now is the time to buy over-the-counter medications; new batteries for your camera, flashlight, and tape recorder; film (ask for a bulk discount if you're buying it at a camera store); sunscreen; water purification pills.

❏ Double-check your gear for such needs as new bootlaces. Waterproof anything that needs it. (You can buy special waterproofing for leather boots and a liquid water repellent for fleece garments.)

❏ Copy all your vital documents in quadruplicate (see page 107). Give two sets—plus your itinerary—to a friend or family member, and ask that person to keep one copy of your file at their office and one at home. That way they can help you even if you call in a panic from halfway around the world on a weekend.

❏ Do a final check on the political situation in the countries you'll be in—those you'll just cross by land and those you'll spend time in. Stay aware of events elsewhere that could have international repercussions, such as terrorists on trial. (For more on keeping abreast of these events, see Chapter 2 and the Appendix.)

❏ Check with the Centers for Disease Control for late-breaking news about any disease outbreaks (see pages 158 and 159). Allow time to get a new prescription (or immunization) if necessary.

❏ Check with your bank's foreign department or the State Department's Bureau of Consular Affairs (see page 159) on the availability of ATMs in the cities you'll be visiting. (In some countries you might not be able to access your bank account.)

❏ Do a packing practice run so you'll know if all your gear will fit in your duffel and daypack.

ONE WEEK BEFORE DEPARTURE

❏ CHECK WITH THE STATE DEPARTMENT FOR ANY LAST-minute advisories or warnings.

❏ If you need it, start taking malaria medication, taking the first dose one week before you'll arrive in *Anopheles* mosquito territory (or according to your doctor's instructions). Try to begin your weekly regimen on a Sunday so you'll be in synch with your group—and less likely to forget.

❏ Spray your clothing and mosquito netting with Permethrin if you will be facing insect threats.

❏ Get the latest currency rates and make a converter chart. For instance, if you're going to Nepal, your instant converter shopping card might look like this:

$$
\begin{aligned}
60 \text{ rupees} &= \$1 \\
120 \text{ rupees} &= \$2 \\
180 \text{ rupees} &= \$3 \\
240 \text{ rupees} &= \$4 \\
300 \text{ rupees} &= \$5 \\
600 \text{ rupees} &= \$10 \\
900 \text{ rupees} &= \$15 \\
1,200 \text{ rupees} &= \$20 \\
1,500 \text{ rupees} &= \$25 \\
3,000 \text{ rupees} &= \$50
\end{aligned}
$$

❏ Pay the balance on your credit card so you'll have the maximum amount available in case of an emergency.

❏ Get cash and traveler's checks. If you're traveling with someone, you might want to get the dual-signature kind, so if one of you is sick or injured midtrip the other will be able to use the checks. How much money should you take? Based on your itinerary, you should have some idea of how often you'll be sightseeing and eating on your own dime. Then consider these other factors:

1. Beverages add up, especially all those bottles of water you'll buy every time you get to a market. Then there's beer or wine in the evenings—even in some of the most remote places—so you might end up with a surprising bar tab.

2. Don't forget all those irresistible crafts and souvenirs you'll want to buy.

3. Remember to include money for tips for your guide and driver, plus tips for one-day guides and drivers at various spots.

4. You'll need airport money: departure taxes plus incidental expenses at all the stops along the way.

5. If your company operates on the "cash kitty" system (an additional amount to be given to the group leader upon arrival), make sure you have that amount set aside (usually in U.S. dollars). And don't forget your handy little bankroll of U.S. one- and five-dollar bills.

6. Bring an amount you feel comfortable with as an emergency backup.

❏ Check your "to do" and "to take" lists for any tasks or items you might have overlooked.

❏ Lay out all your clothing and gear and start packing.

1. Put all your absolute essentials into your daypack—things like prescription medications, camera and film—just in case you're stopped at the boarding gate and told to check your duffel. That way you'll have your "just can't lose" items with you even if you and your duffel are parted for a day or forever.

2. Your absolutely essential clothing should go on board in your daypack or on your body, even if you do look like the Pillsbury doughboy. Put your mittens, balaclava, and knit hat in the pockets of your waterproof jacket—and plan to wear it on board. (If it's too warm to actually wear a jacket, you can just tie it around your waist. It might even come in handy. Cabins are usually cool—sometimes downright chilly—on transoceanic flights).

3. Put your sandals or running shoes in your daypack or tie them to the outside. Plan to wear your hiking boots on board (unless you have plenty of room in your daypack). Once you're on your overseas plane you can get slip on your "comfort" shoes.

❏ Get a haircut.

❏ Reconfirm your flight at least forty-eight hours before departure. Tuck your travel agent's toll-free number in your travel pouch in case you have a problem when you arrive at any airport gate.

ONE DAY BEFORE DEPARTURE

❏ MAKE A LAST-MINUTE CHECK ON THE WEATHER AT your destination, via the Internet or the Weather Channel. Something might have caused an unusual weather pattern—a volcanic eruption—so you'll need clothing for cooler or wetter than normal weather.

❏ Double-check your travel wallet to make sure you have all the essentials—not just the obvious items such as your passport and tickets—but things like your yellow medical certificate stapled to your passport and your phone list of IAMAT doctors.

❑ Do a last-minute check of the contents of your daypack and duffel.

❑ Stick some healthy snacks in your daypack, like trail mix and carrot sticks, so you'll be able to resist the worst of the airline food.

❑ Clip your toenails and file your nails.

❑ Set your alarm.

DAY OF DEPARTURE

❑ CALL YOUR AIRLINE TO CHECK FLIGHT TIMES AND status.

❑ Slap on your Indiana Jones hat and head for the airport.

CHAPTER 10

THE TRIP OF A LIFETIME

INALLY, AFTER ALL THE PLANNING AND SHOPPING AND training, you're set for takeoff. Just remember, little things mean a lot—especially on an adventure travel trip. From the time you leave home until after you return, attention to details will make all the difference.

You should relax and enjoy this trip of a lifetime—but keep your wits about you. Your trip can exceed your wildest expectations, provided you take the proper steps to stay safe, healthy, and happy.

AT THE AIRPORT

WALK AROUND, INSPECT THE BOUTIQUES, PERUSE THE MAGAZINE stands—just stay on your feet as much as you can now, while you're still able. Avoid the bar and even the soda machines. Drink water or fruit juices to give your body a head start in your fight against the high-altitude dehydration ahead.

Buy a liter bottle of water, or fill your own water bottles so you'll have an adequate supply on board, especially for long flights. It's best not to depend on flight attendants to bring you all the liquids you'll need.

IN THE AIR

IF YOU'RE OFF ON A TYPICAL HALFWAY-AROUND-THE-WORLD adventure trip, this could be the longest flight of your life. You could spend about forty-eight hours on planes or in airports. For instance, consider this "typical" adventure trip itinerary: You live in Springfield, Illinois. You'll fly to St. Louis, then to New York, where you'll catch your overnight flight to London. You'll arrive some time the next morning, and that evening you'll spend your second night in a row in an airplane seat, flying from London to Dar es Salaam. Finally, on your third day in transit, you'll fly to Majunga on the island of Madagascar.

By the time you land, ready to begin the trip of a lifetime, you certainly won't be in the best shape of your life. Fatigue, dehydration, and lack of exercise take their toll after twenty-four or forty-eight hours of air travel. Fight fatigue by napping (especially during films, when passengers quiet down and flight attendants and their carts disappear). Pull out your eye shade and ear plugs, settle back, and relax. If you're not in the pricier business class, you can achieve a rough approximation of those recliners by putting your seat back as far as possible and propping your feet up on your daypack. At mealtime, stick to carbohydrates and leave the protein on your tray; pasta, bread, and potatoes should help you nod off.

You'll need to fight two in-flight threats: tight space and dehydration. The long hours you'll spend in a cramped airline seat can, at the least, lead to muscle cramps and lower back pain. At worst, the decrease in circulation to your legs can lead to dangerous blood clots that can put your trip—even your life—in danger. When you're not napping, don't just sit there folded up like an accordion—stretch and exercise regularly. Try to walk an aisle circuit each hour; when you reach the back of the plane you'll probably find space to do some stretching exercises. Back in your seat, roll your head, stretch your arms, move your legs up and down, flex your toes, and tense and relax the muscles in your abdomen and buttocks.

Dehydration, the other major threat, can make you excessively tired and more susceptible to disease. Avoid alcohol and caffeine; stick to juices and water—*lots* of water.

During your wide-awake hours, review your Swahili 101 so you'll be able to hit the streets ready to say the bare minimum: *hello, good-bye, please, thank you, excuse me, I'm sorry, I don't understand Swahili.* Review pronunciation as well. People are wonderfully forgiving when they see that you're trying to say even a word or two in their language, but if your pronunciation doesn't come close, someone might hear *stupid* when you meant *sorry.*

Shortly before any landing, use a nasal decongestant spray (reportedly better than oral decongestants) to help prevent the ear pain that can be so excruciating and last for hours. And, if you brought them, don't forget to insert those pain-prevention devices in your ears.

After you board your last long flight, try to shift to your new time zone. Time your naps to coincide with your new nighttime. Reset your watch and set its alarm for one hour before you're due to land. When it goes off, grab your water bottles and head to the back of the plane to refill with the airline's bottled water. When you land, you'll be too busy trying to get through customs and figuring out where to go next without worrying about finding something safe to drink—and paying for it with local currency.

> ### FOR WOMEN ONLY
> Don't forget the increased risk of blood clotting in your legs if you're pregnant, on birth-control pills, or on hormone-replacement therapy.

ON ARRIVAL

WHEN YOU CHECK IN AT YOUR HOTEL, IF YOU HAVEN'T BEEN met at the airport by a representative from your adventure company you might need to present one of your vouchers. There probably will be a block of rooms already assigned to your group, but if you get a room above the sixth floor, ask for something lower. Six floors is as high as most fire engine ladders go, and safety standards and fire codes in developing countries aren't always the best.

Chances are, even if you've managed to grab some in-flight sleep, you'll be groggy and disoriented. In your condition it's easy to make mistakes. When you get to your hotel room, you'll probably stumble into the bathroom to brush your fuzzy teeth. Stop and think! Tooth brushing is something we all do automatically, absentmindedly turning on the faucet. In this case, that faucet water could be loaded with pathogens—so use your own water supply, even if the hotel has supplied a bottle. (At your evening orientation meeting, your trip leader will brief you on when and where to trust the water.)

Next, you'll want a shower. Stop and think! Keep your mouth shut. In the shower, that is. When that water splashes down on your face, chances are some drops will get in your mouth if you're not careful. You would think nothing of this at home, but when traveling in developing countries it's a good idea to zip your lip.

After you've showered, you might want to flop on your bed and go to sleep. If it's daytime or even early evening, don't! Stay awake; go outside, walk around, make a big effort to get in synch with your new clock, even if your jet-lagged body is begging for a nap. Tuck your compass and the guidebook pages for this city into your pocket and go out and explore whatever exotic new world you've landed in.

Here's something else to tuck in your pocket: something with the hotel's name on it, such as a matchbook. This is doubly important when you're in a country in Asia, where the writing symbols bear no resemblance to the Western alphabet. Showing a taxi driver the name of your hotel written in English might not be any help.

> **TIP**
>
> In many places, you'll have to surrender your passport at the hotel desk when you check in. If this happens, be sure to put one of your photocopies in your travel wallet and keep it with you at all times. Depending on the snatch-and-grab potential where you are, it might be best to put your airline tickets and most of your other travel-wallet items in the hotel safe.

Before you hit the streets, stop at the front desk to ask for a map of the city with the hotel's location marked on it. Then ask the concierge to draw a circle encompassing the hotel and areas in which it's safe to wander. Most foreign cities are safer than big U.S. cities, but it's best to get a scouting report. Get the lowdown on local transportation also. In some cities, for instance, it's not a good idea to get into certain types of taxis.

If you didn't change any currency at the airport, do so at the hotel so you'll have a little walking-around money. Just exchange a small amount, though, because the rate will be higher there than at a bank or cambio. Don't put this cash in your travel wallet—keep that out of sight under your shirt. This way you can just reach in your pocket for local currency (and your converter chart) if you spot something on the street you want to buy.

STREET SMARTS

Be sure to keep your travel wallet out of sight—around your neck or waist, under your shirt or top. Stay aware of your surroundings and be on guard if you're bumped or distracted by someone.

Stay away from any rallies or demonstrations. Even if you're on the periphery of any such crowds, don't take pictures. Your camera might be confiscated.

Look backward as well as forward as you're walking around so you can take note of landmarks to head for when you're ready to go back. Try to keep mentally oriented as to where you are in relation to your hotel.

BACK AT THE HOTEL

After you get back from your walk, you might want to stop at the hotel bar for a celebratory drink. Make it a beer if you do. No matter what they tell you at the bar, don't gamble and go for a mixed drink with ice cubes. Chances are the ice is a frozen version of the water you've been so careful to avoid so far.

Before you turn in for the night, go out in the hallway and check the exits. Make sure you know where the stairs are and that the doors to the stairwells aren't padlocked. Count the number of doors between your room and the stairs and memorize the layout. In case there's a fire, you'll know how to escape despite smoke and darkness. Put your shoes and a flashlight next to your bed and keep your travel wallet in your pillowcase, under your head. Set your watch/alarm so you won't miss breakfast or, worse, sleep so late you're not ready to leave with the group.

> **IT HAPPENED**
>
> The adventure travel group arrived at a glitzy high-rise hotel that looked impressively modern. One woman asked the waiter if the ice cubes were safe and was assured they were. She tossed down two Cuba libres, and the next morning was flat on her back with terrible abdominal pain, in no shape to get on the plane for the next adventure. Months later, after exhaustive testing and excruciating bouts of pain, a travel medicine specialist finally diagnosed the exotic parasite she'd picked up—more than likely in those ice cubes.

EAT, DRINK, AND STAY MERRY

EXERCISE CAUTION EVERY TIME YOU EAT OR DRINK. WHEN you're eating as a group out in the field or in a village, your leader should ensure the safety of your food and drink. But there will be many times when you're on your own.

Stick to food that's steaming hot. Don't eat anything fresh—unless you've peeled it yourself. The general rule when traveling in any undeveloped region: "Peel it, boil it, or

TIP

You don't always have to forego fresh veggies. The salads with the camp meals made by your adventure company's staff should be safe. If the outfit runs a tight ship, they soak salad vegetables in water with disinfectant.

TIP

Wipe off any water on the top of a can or bottle. The same goes for a spoon or the rim of a glass. Infection can be transmitted from a just-washed but still-wet surface. Whatever touches your lips should be clean and dry.

TIP

If you're in a South Pacific or Indian Ocean region, avoid barracuda and puffer fish, which often are toxic. Other fish that are caught on tropical reefs—grouper, snapper, sea bass, and amberjack—also might be poisonous.

forget it." That rules out most fresh fruits and vegetables.

Buy bottled water with an unbroken seal. Carbonated is your best choice: When you see those bubbles you know the water didn't come from a nearby tap or stream. Bottled soft drinks usually are safe, but check with your leader as to brands. (In China, for instance, there have been reports of bacteria and harmful additives in domestic sodas.) And remember, no ice cubes!

Wash your hands in the camp's chlorinated water basin and use your own antibiotic solution or wipes at other times. And take extra care when you're around children—they might appear healthy but could be carrying parasites. Don't let them touch any of your food or utensils.

Avoid milk products—including ice cream. Other foods that could be hazardous: raw fish, undercooked meat, shellfish, and eggs.

SAFEGUARD YOUR HEALTH

On a trip like this, when you're many miles and perhaps many days from any sort of medical expertise, an ounce of prevention isn't worth just a pound of cure—it's worth a ton! Yet travelers who are careful about what they eat and drink can be all too carefree in other ways.

You've done all you should ahead of time: gotten all the right immunizations, packed the right medicines and first-aid items, learned how to stay healthy in primitive conditions. But you can blow all those careful preparations with one careless day.

When you're in a malaria region, stay vigilant and armed. Use your insect repellent. If the thought of intimate contact with a toxic liquid bothers you, remember the alternative: Malaria can kill. And wear your Permethrin-treated clothing at all times. If you're on a longer trip, after two weeks spray your clothing again with Permethrin. Do the same with your mosquito net.

Use that net wherever you sleep if you're in prime malaria

territory. The most dangerous mosquito—*Anopheles*—often attacks between midnight and dawn. Don't be lulled if your room has screens: They could have little holes the invaders could squeeze through, or mosquitoes could have drifted in when outside doors were opened.

Stay hydrated. Drink a pint or so of water in the morning while you're still in camp; then refill your bottle before starting out. Do the same at lunchtime. Even in cold weather you need lots of liquids. If you run out of your supply of safe water and need to use iodine pills, follow the directions carefully. If the water is at all cloudy, double the dose; if it's cold, double the waiting time.

Before you set out for a day's walk, put moleskin on any blister-prone spots on your feet. Once you're on the trail, stop and tighten your boot laces when they get loose. And the minute you feel a "hot spot," stop, take your boot off, and apply antibiotic ointment and moleskin. Don't ignore a blister-in-the-making until the next group rest stop. A blister will hurt and, more dangerously, open the door to infection.

If the group stops by a swimming hole or waterfall, resist the temptation to take that refreshing dip unless you're sure there's no risk of waterborne parasites in that country's fresh-water streams and lakes. And don't stroll barefoot along a river-bank or shoreline either: There could be larvae in the soil that can bore right through unbroken skin and cause something as serious as kidney failure.

As for salt water, here too you might want to think twice. Bays and oceans near cities in regions without strict standards can be heavily polluted.

Stay away from wild animals and domestic pets, even if you're an animal lover. Rabies is prevalent in some popular adventure travel regions, such as India and Thailand. It can be transmitted through a scratch or even a lick from an infected animal. If you do come in contact with an animal and there's cause for concern, scrub and rinse the skin thoroughly and use an antiseptic, then seek medical help. Your leader should have a plan for such contingencies.

Remember your prophylaxis prescriptions. If your doctor has prescribed Diamox for the high altitudes ahead of you, remember to start taking your medication a couple of days before beginning your ascent. And don't forget your weekly antimalarial pills.

TIP

If your urine is darker than pale yellow, you're not drinking enough fluids.

TIP

Infrequently, Pepto-Bismol causes temporary side effects that shouldn't alarm you: blackening of stools and ringing in the ears. But don't take Pepto-Bismol if you're taking aspirin or a blood thinner such as Coumadin.

TIP

If you develop any serious medical troubles, the U.S. embassy should have a list of doctors and try to make sure you get good care. And in a case of suspected rabies they'll also know how to find a safe, reliable supply of vaccine (you'll need some even if you've had the preliminary shots).

TRAVELER'S DIARRHEA

To ward off "turista"—the diarrhea that plagues about one in five travelers to Africa, Asia, and South America—some doctors advise a regimen of Pepto-Bismol tablets. Travelers on the preventive plan take one to two tablets four times a day for a maximum of three weeks.

If you do develop intestinal troubles—in some places it's quite common despite vigilant preventive measures—try taking Pepto-Bismol tablets and drink plenty of fluids. Even if you have only a mild case, take some oral rehydration solution. If you run out of prepared mixes, you can concoct a substitute that is less effective but better than nothing: Mix eight teaspoons of sugar and one-half teaspoon of salt in one quart of water.

Antimotility medications will stop the diarrhea because they stop the contractions of your intestines. This always is an attractive alternative when you're in desperate straits in the midst of a trip, but it could be counterproductive. Doctors often advise against taking something that will trap infecting organisms and give them more time to multiply. It's sometimes better to let those germs move on out—unless you're facing a day with a long bus or plane ride.

Some doctors say you should take an antibiotic, such as ciprofloxacin, in cases of intestinal problems, particularly if you have a fever. If you have severe nausea and vomiting with a high temperature, consult the medical information you brought with you.

If you're in a malaria region and develop fever, chills, headache, and malaise, you'll need immediate medical attention, including a blood test. If you're more than a day away from such help, and if malaria is suspected, you might need to take your emergency Fansidar, if it was prescribed by your travel doctor.

HIGH PLACES REVISITED

WHEN YOU'RE TREKKING IN THE MOUNTAINS, THE HIGHER you go, the more extreme the conditions. The sun's rays become

4 percent stronger with each 1,000 feet of elevation gain. The temperature drops, usually at least three degrees for every 1,000 feet—but you'll feel colder because the wind will pick up, especially as you go above the tree line. And the more you need your muscles, the worse they'll feel; they'll be crying out for oxygen when there's less available for your lungs to take in.

If your trip is taking you to new heights, the following tips will help you avoid problems:

- Apply sunscreen liberally and often. Cover your arms and legs and shade your face. Wear sunglasses.
- Drink copious amounts of water or juice—about four quarts of liquid a day. Drink frequently, even if you're not thirsty. The higher you go, the drier the air and the faster your body loses moisture. (Even if you're not obviously losing water through sweating, you're losing it in your breath.)
- Make sure your urine stays pale.
- Avoid caffeine and alcohol. They're diuretics and will flush your system.
- Acetazolamide (Diamox) can help those who are prone to altitude sickness. It works best if you start taking it two days before starting to climb. And if you're taking it, remember to double your efforts to stay hydrated.
- Keep your body nourished with a steady stream of complex carbohydrates. Cut back on the fats and proteins, since they require more oxygen to metabolize. And don't add extra salt to your food.
- If the grade is steep and your breath is short, try the "rest step" technique: Take smaller steps, and with each one pause momentarily while your back leg is straight and still bearing your weight.
- Don't take any sleeping aids. Such pills could slow your breathing and lead to altitude sickness.
- Avoid getting chilled. Cover your head and add layers as the temperature drops. Microfleece and your windbreaker/rain gear will keep you warm even in severe conditions.
- Watch for symptoms of acute mountain sickness: headache, dizziness, loss of appetite, weakness, cough, persistent yawning, and hyperventilation. These are yellow-flag warnings, signs that you should acclimatize to the new altitude before going any higher. They're also

a sign that things could get much worse if you ignore them and keep on trekking onward and upward.

- Be alert for symptoms of HAPE and HACE—those potentially fatal conditions. Severe fatigue, vomiting, severe headache, and loss of coordination indicate cerebral edema. Severe cough, shortness of breath, watery or bloody sputum, noisy breathing, and severe fatigue are signs of pulmonary edema. Do not engage in wishful thinking and minimize the importance of these symptoms. It's up to you to monitor your body and let your leader know immediately if you're in trouble.

Remember: The only life-saving treatment for HAPE and HACE is *immediate* descent to an altitude where the symptoms dissipate. The leader should be prepared for such an emergency and arrange for one of the porters to help you back down. If your trip is equipped with a Gamow bag—which simulates a 5,000-foot altitude—your leader could ease your symptoms before you descend.

BEATING THE HEAT

AT LOWER LEVELS IN HOT CLIMATES, BE ON THE LOOKOUT for signs of heat exhaustion—primarily dizziness, weakness, and headache. The combination of high heat and high humidity is dangerous. Moisture-laden air prevents your sweat from evaporating and cripples your body's cooling system. Liquids, shade, and rest spell relief.

> **TIP**
>
> The older you are, the more careful you have to be in the heat. With each passing decade you sweat less, so you can't cool down as well as you once did.

If your skin turns dry and hot and your face gets very red, you might be close to heat stroke, which is much more dangerous than heat exhaustion. As with advanced altitude sickness, immediate treatment is a must. Get your body cooled somehow, either by immersing yourself in water (forget about water flukes at this point) or getting people to pour water over your body, especially your head.

SAFETY TIPS

If you're cycling:

- Always wear your helmet, regardless of the surface, and make sure you put it on correctly—down over your forehead, not pushed back on your head.

- Adjust the strap for a snug fit.
- Wear sunglasses to protect your eyes from branches, insects, or dirt particles.

On a trek:

- If you leave the trail to duck behind trees or rocks to relieve yourself, leave your cap or pack on the trail. That way, those coming along will know where you are and you won't get left behind.
- Check the ground carefully when you go off into the brush—you don't want to stumble into a close encounter with a poisonous snake or other critter. If you're hiking in pit viper territory, let the guides take the lead!

On the bus:

- Don't sit in the very front or the very back—sit near an exit or an open window. (Some companies use public transportation to move the group from city to city. On many third world buses, the brakes and steering are questionable—and the same is true of the oncoming vehicles. There's a reason why those visors and dashboards are filled with religious symbols!)
- If you have to put your duffel in an outside luggage compartment, wrap it in garbage bags and secure it with some sort of colorful ribbon or tape to distinguish it from the other baggage.
- During the ride, remember what your mother told you: Don't take candy from strangers. There have been reports of travelers being sedated and robbed by fellow passengers.

> **TIP**
>
> Safeguard your boots. If you're visiting a mosque or a shrine and have to take your boots off, put them in your daypack if there's no attendant who'll watch them (for a fee). And don't leave them outside the door when you're sleeping, either. And as long as you're keeping track of your gear, don't let your sunglasses get away. With a sports strap you'll always have them—either on your nose or around your neck.

SHOPPING SENSE

MAYBE YOU'VE HEARD RETURNING TRAVELERS COMPLAIN about shopping in the developing country they visited—how aggressive and persistent the shopkeepers and street vendors were. But this won't be so unpleasant if you remember that you're in a different country where they do things differently. Just accept the custom and reply—with a smile—*no, thank you* or *no money*, in their language. This friendly but firm approach works much better than ignoring their overtures or responding rudely.

As for bargaining, you need to tread a fine line between playing the fool and exacting too dear a price. Some give-and-take is usually expected, and your trip leader should be able to give you reasonable guidelines, something like, "expect to get about one-third off the starting price." But be careful, because one sale can mean much to a family in a country where the per capita annual income might be less than you spent on the clothes you're wearing. Leave the vendor with his or her dignity and a reasonable profit.

If you buy clothing or jewelry, find out the proper way to wear it. Your guide should be able to show you what would be appropriate and what would be disrespectful.

Resist the temptation to buy antique items. Some countries don't have a Paul Mellon to buy a collection of treasures and build a museum for them. By not buying an antique pot or sacred icon, you'll be helping to preserve that country's history for future generations.

Everyone wants to bring home souvenirs. And everyone knows carved ivory and big-cat furs are off limits. But that tortoise-shell jewelry could have come from an endangered sea turtle, that black-coral jewelry from a living reef that regrows at the rate of one-tenth of an inch a year. Even if something isn't on the forbidden list, think about the long-term consequences of supporting the harvesting and selling of such items as snake, sea turtle, or crocodile products; birds or bird feathers; orchids, cacti, or any rare plants; or anteater leather. As the World Wildlife Fund advises, avoid "anything made from hides, shells, feathers, or teeth." Research the relevant customs regulations also, so you won't buy something that will in turn be confiscated either when you leave the country or when you reenter the United States.

FAREWELL TIME

NOW YOU CAN BE A LITTLE MORE DARING IF you're so inclined. Follow the leader's suggestions for reliable street-stall cooks and sample the life of a native—as long as the food is steaming hot. But don't order any mixed drinks with ice!

> **TIP**
>
> Normally, your leader will reconfirm everyone's international flight. If this isn't the case, call your airline three days ahead of departure.

BACK HOME

WHEN IT'S ALL OVER AND YOU'RE BACK IN FAMILIAR SUR-
roundings, don't let your guard down completely. Keep taking
your weekly malaria pills for the recommended time period.
And remember that you might have brought home some unfamiliar maladies.

If you get flu symptoms or intestinal pains—even months
later—see a doctor and tell her or him exactly where you've
been. Some of those exotic pathogens just bide their time
before striking, and you could be coming down with something serious.

CHAPTER 11

THE WELL-TEMPERED TRAVELER

O N AN ADVENTURE TRAVEL TRIP YOU'LL BE THROWN together with a group of strangers. And then you'll encounter strange cultures. You can do your part to make the experience an enjoyable one for everyone involved—your group, the people you meet, and yourself—if you follow a few guidelines.

YOUR NEW FAMILY

AN ADVENTURE TRAVEL GROUP IS SOMEWHAT LIKE A LARGE family on vacation. There are ways to get along with each other, even in cramped quarters and uncomfortable situations.

Be on time whenever you're supposed to move on or move out. It's rude to keep the rest of the group waiting, and they'll resent you if it happens repeatedly. It will help if you develop a routine. If you're not a morning person, organize for the next day the night

138

before. Plan ahead and make sure you have what you'll need in your daypack. Depending on the weather, terrain, and a host of other variables, you'll need:

- insect repellent
- sunglasses
- sunscreen and lip screen
- water bottles
- water pills and flavoring
- food bars
- tissues or toilet paper
- extra Ziplocs (large and small)
- camera, film, lenses, filters, lens tissues
- hat and/or balaclava
- extra layers
- rain gear
- moleskin and blister pads
- hiking pole
- flashlight
- first-aid kit
- emergency items: compass, map, whistle, space blanket

Clean your camera lenses and filters at night. In the morning, get organized while breakfast is cooking. Fill your water bottles, drink some, and refill. Apply sunscreen. Do a last-minute check of your daypack.

> **TIP**
>
> Always keep one needle/syringe in your daypack in case you're severely injured during the day and evacuated with only your daypack.

Wash up carefully before handling group utensils. You don't want to spread trouble to your fellow trekkers. If yours is a less-than-soft trip and you're assigned to camp chores, such as helping with the cooking or dishwashing, follow the leader's explicit instructions. The health of the entire group could depend on it.

Take only a reasonable portion on your first trip through the food line, even if you're famished. Usually you can go back for seconds, but there might be times when there's only enough for one helping each, and in that case you don't want the last person through the line to be scraping the bowls.

Don't think of the staff—driver, cooks, porters—as servants. They're members of your temporary family, too. Treat them with the same courtesy as you do your fellow group members. Learn their names right away. Say *good morning, please,* and *thank you*—in their language. If they speak some

English (or another language you speak well), talk to them, ask questions, show an interest in their lives and their knowledge of the area.

Show appreciation for the goat or whatever other animal is in the stew. Don't make any disparaging remarks that would hurt the feelings of the crew—even if you think they're out of earshot.

When there's a temporary new member of the crew—a driver or a local guide—remember to express your appreciation, both verbally and monetarily. (One some trips, all such tips are included, in which case say good-bye with a smile and *very good, thank you very much* in the local language.)

Stay good-natured in the face of discomfort and adversity. You'll make it easier on others and on yourself.

ECO-ETIQUETTE

WHEN THERE'S NOT EVEN A PRIMITIVE LATRINE, PRACTICE proper backcountry sanitation and bury the waste. That means digging your own minilatrine at least a hundred yards from any water source. Some travel companies supply trowels, but if it's on your recommended packing list, be sure to bring one. Put all refuse—toilet paper, tampons, sanitary napkins—in a Ziploc to be disposed of properly at camp or in town.

Do all your washing and tooth brushing at least fifty feet from any watercourse, and use your biodegradable soap. Be very careful not to contaminate any springs, and dispose of waste water far away from any water source or course.

Be quiet and unobtrusive in wildlife areas. Noise and sudden movements might scare animals and birds away and spoil the wilderness experience for the others.

Carry your American-style refuse—dead batteries, empty toothpaste tubes, razor blades (anything the villagers can't burn safely after you're gone)—in Ziplocs. Dispose of it when you reach a place where such things can be dealt with properly. Always have a trash bag with you on the trail.

"Take only pictures, leave only footprints"—that hikers' creed is a good motto for adventure travelers. Leave the landscape as you found it, without picking plants or pocketing shells, and without a trace of litter or waste. Don't be a looter—don't pick up artifacts at ruins; leave them in their natural setting for others to see or for archaeologists to study.

Stay on trails or pathways. Blazing shortcuts can damage fragile vegetation and cause erosion.

If you're about to embark on an island with its own unique ecosystem, check your cuffs and pockets carefully to make sure you won't distribute seeds that could introduce alien species.

A GOOD ATTITUDE

THIS SHOULD BE THE TIME OF YOUR LIFE. RELAX, HAVE FUN, go with the flow. That's a tall order for some Type A personalities (the ones who usually have an agenda: lose five pounds on this trek, bag some peaks, take a thousand show-and-tell photos).

Think twice about constantly using your camera. That equipment can come between you and an optimum experience. All too often, the photo buffs are fussing and focusing, viewing a small square instead of drinking in the whole spectacle. Spend some time just looking and savoring. At some photo-ops, leave your camera in your pack and just enjoy the astounding sights you've come so far to experience. While others zoom in on one animal, you'll soak in the whole herd of giraffes—how they nibble on the acacia trees, how they lope gracefully through the veldt. This is the scene that will live on in your memory far more vividly than any still photo.

There are other ways to capture experiences. Remember to turn on your tape recorder whenever there's a memorable sound—birds, animals, native songs, musical instruments, vendors' cries, market clamor. And before you turn in at night, write in your journal, even if it's just a sentence or two capturing the essence of the day. When you get home you'll be glad you took the time. Those details and impressions can bring back the clarity of the experience more than most photos will.

Be flexible, tolerant, and patient, especially when things don't go according to plan. When you were told to expect the unexpected, that included encounters with third world systems and cultures. Banish any expectations of efficiency, timeliness, and "proper procedures." People in other parts of the world have different concepts of time than you do and often just don't understand your Western tendency to hurry.

When problems arise—delays, breakdowns—try to keep your mouth shut and your eyes and mind open. Don't let annoyance blind you to the unfolding drama around you. Just view this as another chance to observe more fascinating details of a different culture or environment.

As for accommodations, you can't expect Western standards or amenities. Don't be like the tourist who complained to the leader, "This isn't even up to Motel 6 standards." You've paid a princely sum for all this, but adopt the attitude of a guest and be gracious.

Meals should be enjoyable occasions. Beef hearts and yak hoofs are part of the adventure—don't predispose your taste buds to reject strange foods. And forget worrying about your weight. Since your trip involves a lot of active participation, you won't go home bulging and bloated even if you do indulge yourself.

MEET AND GREET

FOR MANY PEOPLE, THE MOST MEMORABLE MOMENTS OF their adventure trips are the cultural interactions. Making genuine connections with people is easy, even if you can't speak more than ten words of the language. Expect to be treated with kindness, and you will be.

Children often break the ice, with the adults following more shyly behind. Your young visitors will slowly drift to the periphery of your lunch circle or tent camp, watching from the fringes. Welcome them with a smile and a wave, then use gestures, drawings, pantomime, body language. Take out your Koosh ball and gesture a toss to get them to play catch. Play your kazoo or sing a few verses of a song. Draw a picture in the dirt or in your notebook.

As for gifts, it's best not to give anything. You'll never have enough for everyone, and someone who starts passing out favors is immediately surrounded like the Pied Piper. And it's inappropriate to give things that won't burn or decompose—such as plastic pens or rubber balloons—to people with no alternative means of trash disposal. Definitely don't pass out sweets to children. Candy quickly rots teeth in places where there's no fluoride or dental care. If you really want to come bearing gifts, bring supplies for the schools and monasteries—pens, paper, crayons, maps, postcards, picture books.

In villages and towns, don't travel in a "pack" with your group. You'll have a much better chance for one-on-one interchanges with the local people if you're alone (or with one companion). Ask your leader about market days so you won't miss these colorful gatherings.

MS. MANNERS

SOME "UGLY AMERICANS" PASS THROUGH NATIVE SETTLE-ments as if they were strolling through a museum of mannequins. They stare and point as if the people were inanimate displays rather than humans with feelings. Yet these same travelers would be insulted and annoyed if a group of foreign tourists turned the tables, stopping in front of their suburban homes, pointing, laughing, and taking pictures.

Also, such tourists often assume that "those people" couldn't possibly know any English. They don't realize that a disparaging remark—"Can you believe they eat this stuff?"—might be understood by the person behind the stall. It's surprising how often there's a knowledge of English, even in remote areas.

Traveling with sensitivity and tolerance will enrich your experience and endear you to the people you meet. Smile, nod, and say hello when you pass on the street or trail. Talk to the locals as much as possible. Even if you ramble on in English and they do the same in Quechua, with smiles and gestures you can communicate friendship, if not much factual information.

Follow local customs. Cover as much of your body as do the people in your host country. Very often this will mean a long-sleeved shirt, long skirt or pants, loose clothing, perhaps a head covering. And show respect and appreciation for a different way of life. You might think a woman's earlobes, grossly enlarged by massive earrings, are grotesque. Yet she might be thinking that your earlobes are pitifully small, your earrings pathetically plain.

If you're lucky enough to be invited into a home, respect the dignity of that family and show appreciation to your hosts. Don't turn down an opportunity to visit because you're squeamish. You might miss the most fascinating opportunity of your trip.

Make sure you know the local etiquette—including gestures—or you might easily unwittingly commit some offensive social gaffes. In many countries it's rude to offer, receive, or eat something with your left hand. For instance, in Nepal it's not polite to pat a child on the head; walk counterclockwise around a shrine; sit with the soles of your feet showing; leave your shoes crossed or flipped (instead of neatly side by side) when you enter

IT HAPPENED

On an East African camping trip, the head of a village invited two visitors into his home. After crawling through a narrow mud tunnel, they entered the thatched structure where a baby lay—with flies covering its eyes and lips. No one in the group moved to wave the flies away, something they might have done instinctively at home. Good thing they didn't—the chief proudly pointed out all the flies on his baby's face, saying "The more flies as a baby, the more children as an adult."

TIP

Some companies are thorough and include information about local customs and etiquette in their pretrip information packets. Some send these packets out months ahead of time, giving you time to prepare, while others wait until the last minute. If your company says it doesn't have the packet for your trip yet, ask for a copy of last year's tips and instructions.

a home; or express admiration for what someone is wearing (making that person feel he or she must give it to you).

CANDID CAMERAS

TAKING GOOD SHOTS IN A FOREIGN CULTURE CAN INVOLVE more than f-stops and focal points. Certain subjects could be forbidden—from schools to temples to people. Even a scenic shot might get you in trouble if there's a bridge in your viewfinder. The government might prohibit you from taking photos of anything related to the military—including everything from border posts to post offices. Airports, hospitals, and industrial sites also are on some no-photo lists.

As for aiming your camera at people, first make sure you aren't in a country where taking pictures conflicts with social custom or religious beliefs. Even if your guidebook and your guide say it's all right, approach your subjects with courtesy. Smile, gesture with your camera, and ask *okay?* in their language before you point and shoot.

If it's cold, keep your camera (or batteries) in a pocket close to your body; if it's dusty, keep your camera in a sealed Ziploc. In general, keep your photo equipment out of sight as much as possible. If your trip involves an internal flight, don't forget to get your camera hand-inspected if you're midway through a roll. Be prepared with some currency in case you have to say *thanks* with more than a smile.

THE END OF THE LINE

MAKE SURE YOU HAVE CASH READY FOR THE FAREWELL gifts for the trip leader and staff. If you've done your homework, you'll know how much this should be for your trip. Tip amounts vary by length of time and size of staff—and of course, by your degree of appreciation.

Once you're home, remember to show your appreciation for the wonders you've seen. Join an international conservation organization. Give money to groups that help third world women become literate and self sufficient. And when you give your "what I did on my vacation" slide show, ask your friends to support nonprofits that are working to save children, ecosystems, and rainforests.

CHAPTER 12

WHAT'S AHEAD
FOR ADVENTURE TRAVELERS?

THE FUTURE LOOKS BRIGHT FOR VACATIONERS WHO WANT to venture into extraordinary realms. Companies are responding to the increasing demand for adventure travel by offering many trips to more places, with itineraries to suit an expanding range of ages, abilities, and interests. There are, however, a few dark clouds in this sunny forecast.

GO NOW
(BEFORE IT DISAPPEARS)

THE MASSIVE, ONGOING LOSS OF THE WORLD'S SPECIES AND rainforests has fearsome long-term consequences for the earth's biodiversity and balance of nature. This destruction of ecosystems also has immediate consequences for adventure travel, as once-beautiful and naturally rich destinations fall victim to the chain saw and the cement mixer.

Each year some thirty million to fifty-five million acres of the world's forests are destroyed. Slash-and-burn devastation is particularly rampant in some of the world's most lush and unspoiled places.

As forests shrink, so will the appeal of many adventure travel destinations. Parks that are tiny oases in the midst of cattle farms and sprawling development cannot offer the wild vistas and clean air of a truly remote sanctuary. And the many species that need a wide expanse of territory to survive will vanish from a habitat bisected by concrete and steel, highways and clear-cuts.

Another danger threatens the extinction of some of the world's most spectacular species: Poachers are killing the wild animals of Africa at an alarming rate. The numbers of elephants and rhinos in some of the prime viewing areas are declining rapidly as poachers elude with ease the small corps of ill-equipped park personnel. The black rhinoceros is a dramatic example of what is happening: In 1970 there were about 60,000; by 1990 there were about 3,000. By the middle of the nineties there were fewer than 200, according to naturalists' estimates.

Regions under the ax or the gun include some of the world's best destinations, the ones that have been at the top of most adventure travelers' wish lists for decades. These trips have achieved "classic" status, with itineraries that offer breathtaking scenery and fascinating culture in one package. Here are just a few examples, beginning with a country that many hoped would lead the way in showing developing countries how to save their habitats and species.

- **Costa Rica.** Hailed as a shining example of how eco-tourism can be successfully managed, Costa Rica has shown that forests could be worth more as parks for tourists than as fields for cattle. Yet, despite the country's stability and relative wealth, the government has been forced to divert funds from preservation to more pressing needs such as roads and hospitals. Clear-cutting continues at an alarming pace, and conservationists report a grave loss of wildlife to poachers: "empty forests" without animals and sea turtle nests without eggs. At Costa Rica's crown jewel national park, the number of guards was cut by 75 percent; on one of the beaches where the endangered leatherneck turtle lays its eggs, only a mile or so is patrolled, leaving the rest of the coastline vulnerable to poachers.

- **Madagascar.** This remote island off the coast of Africa has more unique indigenous plants and animals than any other country in the world. People travel halfway around the globe to see its lemurs, orchids, and cuckoo rollers. But large areas of virgin forest have been cut, and the remaining forests—and species habitats—are threatened by development.
- **East Africa.** The poaching of elephants and rhinos is continuing, with rangers still ill equipped and outnumbered. Another threat is intertribal warfare, including recent atrocities in a region that once offered rare opportunities to view gorillas in the wild.
- **Nepal.** Deforestation is an increasing problem here. The population is growing rapidly—and along with it, the need for firewood.

Take heed if these places—or others similarly threatened—are in your travel dreams. Don't make the mistake of putting off your choice trip indefinitely, like a bottle of fine wine sitting on your rack until you're ready for it.

GO NOW
(BEFORE EVERYBODY ELSE GETS THERE)

AN INFLUX OF TOURISTS INEVITABLY ALTERS AN ISOLATED people and pollutes their culture, and the support systems that develop for visitors scar the landscape. Popularity inevitably breeds amenities and infrastructure, modernization and development.

And tourism is only a small factor. All over the world, countries that once existed in relative isolation are changing rapidly. The pace has accelerated drastically with the advent of the global economy. The pressure is on to turn forests into ranches, build sprawling industrial complexes, and pave roads into remote areas.

The communications revolution is another factor, with cell phones and satellite dishes now cropping up in primitive areas. Traditional values are diluted as Western ideas filter in, and cultures are changed irrevocably.

For instance, tourism in Nepal has increased more than 200 percent in the last decade, and the foreign crowds are leaving their imprint, both physically and culturally. Travelers on Nepal's much-loved, much-traveled Annapurna circuit route report Western litter along the trails and American blow-'em-ups playing on VCRs in the villages. Mention Bali or Belize, and there are travelers who say, "Ah, but you should have seen it years ago, before everyone started going there."

There are countries, however, where this has not yet happened, or if tourism is causing changes, the influence is barely perceptible. When a new country opens to tourism or when a popular country opens a new area to trekking, it offers a once-in-a-lifetime chance to experience a pristine world.

When this happens, go quickly, when the only other people you'll see will be pilgrims and villagers in traditional garb. This is an opportunity to experience an exotic area untouched by tourism—the ultimate in adventure travel. If this sounds like your kind of trip, consider these new places that are showing up in catalogs—future Balis, perhaps, but for now relatively unspoiled and undeveloped.

- **Panama.** This country is just opening up to wilderness travel. One company features a trek that retraces the route of the explorer Balboa when he discovered the Pacific Ocean. With adventure travel in its infancy here, there's a chance to see a land of rich biological diversity and flourishing indigenous groups as unspoiled as Costa Rica was a decade or so ago.

- **Vietnam.** Another recent entry to adventure travel lists, a growing number of companies combine trips to its unspoiled beaches and lush highlands with visits to hill tribes and villages where the culture is said to still be intact, having survived everything from colonial rule to civil war. But travel advisers say this will be a very different country within the decade because of the expected flood of tourist and investment dollars.

- **Bhutan.** This is a fairly recent entry in adventure company catalogs. Today's travelers will find it unspoiled thanks to the current government's restrictive policies designed to preserve the culture and the landscape. Bhutan limits tourist visas, only letting about 750 travelers per week into a country the size of Switzerland. And its laws require wearing traditional dress—this is one destination where you're not likely to enter a village filled with people wearing tourist-castoff Chicago Bulls T-shirts.

- **Nepal.** This popular country is opening areas previously closed to Western travelers. Routes are now available in its pristine eastern region, giving trekkers a chance to see the country the way it used to be.
- **India.** New mountainous regions have opened here as well. Adventure travel companies are taking trekkers through valleys and mountains in two eastern provinces that until very recently had been off limits to foreign travelers.

There are a number of other opportunities to get in on the ground floor. The Nubra Valley in Ladakh opened just two years ago. Laos, the least-developed country in Southeast Asia, is no longer closed to foreigners. Routes through ancient Persia are now available in Iran. Companies are able to take travelers to Sikkim and Mongolia, and along Silk Road routes from Pakistan to places like Tashkent and Samarkand. Burma and Cambodia also have opened up to adventure travel, although security is a problem due to continuing political instability.

Brand-new destinations will be cropping up in company catalogs. Surinam, for instance, could be a future candidate. This former Dutch colony on the coast of South America has more than 250 species of tropical plants per square mile, and its rainforest is one of the world's most biologically diverse habitats.

There are trade-offs, of course, when you decide to go on one of the early trips to a newly opened region or country. These new trips are more subject to those expect-the-unexpected glitches, and they might not run as smoothly or as safely as later ones will.

But if you want to go to the most pristine and unspoiled places, *carpe diem.* Go now to those spots that have recently opened to travelers—and keep your eyes open for the next ones.

GO NOW
(BEFORE THE WAR)

OR BEFORE THE RIOTS, THE REVOLUTION, THE CRIME WAVE, or the next terrorist insurgency.

Seeing threatened regions while they're still teeming with wildlife isn't the only reason to go now. Political turmoil and civil war can seal off a prime adventure travel destination just as effectively as the Iron Curtain once did.

Keep an eye on the international news. When you read about an incipient radical movement in a country you hope to explore "some day," you might want to readjust your timetable in order to go while a stable government is still in charge (and still able to keep things safe for travelers).

Even internally peaceful countries can be troubled by spillover violence from neighbors. Insurgent uprisings often spread across national boundaries, and the area you hope to explore might be next door to a country wracked by dangerous civil unrest. Fabled Morocco, for instance, with its souks, medinas, desert camel rides, and Berber village treks, borders bleeding Algeria.

Pay attention to economic trends. The appealing adventure travel areas can be adversely affected in a country where a development boom is steamrolling along. The building and paving might send its tentacles way beyond city centers, changing the character of the people and the countryside.

A serious reversal in a country's economic fortunes can spur a frightening crime wave. When there's a currency devaluation followed by skyrocketing inflation, people get desperate. With no alternatives, they turn to crime, and tourists are likely and profitable targets. What happened in Mexico City is illustrative: The peso was devalued in 1994; crime rose 36 percent in 1995 and 14 percent more in 1996.

Watch out for Southeast Asia. If a country there is on your dream list, it might be a good idea to move it to the top of the "go before it's too late" list. Something similar to the Mexico City situation might develop in some of Southeast Asia's popular adventure travel destinations in the wake of the dramatic collapse of so many economies there.

VOTING WITH YOUR DOLLARS

TRUE ECOTOURISM ATTEMPTS TO FOLLOW A COMBINATION OF the physicians' credo, "First do no harm," and the hikers' motto, "Take only pictures, leave only footprints." Supporting adventure travel companies that adhere to the principles of ecotourism might help save some destinations. When your dollars go to a company that treads lightly and puts money back into local hands, you're supporting the conservation of that country.

Despite its problems, Costa Rica remains a successful example of an economic transition. Its government recognizes tourism as its main source of income and it attempts to implement policies that preserve the resources that attract tourists. Not only have Costa Rican forests been preserved, but the money left in the wake of nature tours proves to other countries that forests can have greater value if left uncut.

Nature safaris in Africa pay for more game wardens to protect wildlife from poachers. In many countries, local people have opened businesses such as galleries, restaurants, lodges, and riding stables in the areas surrounding national parks. And in some areas (like the savanna of Guyana in South America), cattle ranchers are exploring ecotourism as an alternative way to generate income.

Of course, it would be naive to think that groups of Westerners regularly descending on remote cultures and traversing wild landscapes could pass through like wisps of vapor. But the most responsible companies try to adhere to the definition of ecotourism: organizing travel to natural areas in a way that conserves the environment and sustains the well-being of local people.

The bottom line: Voting with your dollars by supporting ecotourism might arrest—or even reverse—actions that have been despoiling a country's cultures and environment.

WHAT'S AHEAD: SPECIALIZED ITINERARIES

TRAVEL EXPERTS FORESEE AN INCREASE IN THE NUMBER OF itineraries offered by adventure travel companies eager to serve the growing range of ages and interests. Some of these groups include:

- **Busy professionals.** More short trips will be offered so that time-pressed professionals can pack a one-week, far-flung adventure into their schedules.
- **Soft-adventure seekers.** As more and more baby boomers move into their fifties and sixties, expect an even greater smorgasbord of soft adventures, with more at-home comforts in the remote wilds.
- **Women only.** More companies are responding to the demand for women's trips. Participants say they find greater support and encouragement, less competition and friction in these all-female groups. Another plus: Traveling without men enables these groups to interact more freely with the women in the more sheltered societies of many developing countries.
- **Families.** Many adventure travel trips are appealing to

a wide range of family members, from grandparents to pre-adolescents. Companies will offer more trips designed especially for families, with itineraries that will feature less driving time, higher safety levels, less-remote locations, radio communication, and guides who also are parents. Look for more adults-with-teenagers trips and grandparents-and-grandchildren trips.

- **Seniors.** For the growing numbers of fit and adventure-some seniors, there will be more trips for those fifty years old and older that feature walks "at a comfortable pace," with accommodations, travel conditions, and exposure to the elements all on a correspondingly softer level.

- **Outdoors jocks.** For those with a yen for a variety of activities there will be more multisport adventure travel trips. One company already is offering such trips, with various combinations of hiking, biking, kayaking, rafting, skiing, and even heli-hiking.

MORE SPECIALTY TRIPS

Trips that cater to special interests also are growing in popularity:

- **Photography tours.** Some of the world's premier photographers are teaming up with adventure travel companies to lead special shutterbug trips. These itineraries are chosen for their photo opportunities, with stops at the most colorful and picturesque spots. The timing is planned to take advantage of the best light, so that the group doesn't arrive at one of the best sights in the harsh noon sun. The pacing is much slower than the normal tour so photographers have plenty of time to frame and focus.

- **Expedition cruises.** Instead of Love Boats with casinos, cabarets, fashion shows, and midnight buffets, these trips offer comfortable amenities coupled with intense education and active exploration. By day, passengers transfer to land in small rubber boats called Zodiacs and take hikes; at night they listen to lectures or watch slide shows narrated by specialists such as biologists or ornithologists. The ships are much smaller than normal cruise ships—a hundred passengers or fewer—and they can maneuver into narrow passages and tiny inlets where big ships never could. This sometimes is the best way to see islands with poor roads and transportation systems that are notorious for breakdowns and delays—as well as the only way to see regions like Antarctica and the Galapagos.

- **Volunteer vacations.** These "do-gooder" trips are like a two-week Peace Corps stint. You can join an ongoing project and do such things as teach English, count animals, build a school, excavate ancient ruins, or record local storytellers. These trips offer unique opportunities to interact with indigenous people and experience family and tribal life in a culture still relatively untouched by outside influences. Humanitarian organizations, conservation organizations, and university research groups organize and staff these trips with professionals, and they welcome volunteers to work alongside. In most cases, the entire cost of such trips, including the airfare, is tax-deductible.
- **Exploratory trips.** You can push the envelope a bit, capture the flavor of a real exploration, help open new windows on more wonders of the world. Some companies want clients along when they experiment with new routes and new countries. Nothing's guaranteed except even more of the unexpected nature of adventure travel, with an extra dose of excitement and challenge.
- **Rugged overland journeys.** Generally for those between the ages of eighteen and forty-five, these trips take groups in trucks or buses on transcontinental trips that last as long as seven months (such as one from Alaska to Tierra del Fuego). If you can only get away for six months, there's a trip from Kathmandu to Southern Africa.

With such a wealth of choices, you should have no trouble finding a trip that's just right for you—and one that's right for the people you'll visit. Now that you know how to choose the best company and how to stay safe and healthy, you should be able to successfully take that trip of a lifetime. And come home and start planning for your next one.

Mark Twain could have been talking about adventure travel when he gave this advice: "Twenty years from now you will be more disappointed by the things you didn't do than by the ones you did do. So throw off the bowlines. Sail away from the safe harbor. . . . Explore. Dream. Discover."

RESOURCES

ADVENTURE TRAVEL COMPANIES

A Sampling of Companies with Itineraries in Exotic Regions of Asia, Africa, and Latin America

Abercrombie & Kent:
800-323-7308

Above the Clouds Trekking:
800-233-4499

Adventure Center:
800-227-8747

Asian Trans-Pacific Journeys (formerly Bolder Adventures):
800-642-2742

Backroads:
800-245-3874

Butterfield & Robinson:
800-678-1147

Geographic Expeditions:
800-777-8183

Himalayan Travel:
800-225-2380

Journeys International:
800-255-8735

Mountain Travel—Sobek:
800-227-2384

Overseas Adventure Travel:
800-221-0814

REI Adventures:
800-622-2236

Sierra Club Outings:
415-977-5630

Wilderness Travel:
800-368-2794

Wildland Adventures:
800-345-4453

Nature Trips

Ecotour Expeditions:
800-688-1822

Field Guides, Inc. (worldwide birding tours):
800-728-4953

Friends of the National Zoo, Washington, D.C.:
202-673-4613

International Expeditions:
800-633-4734

National Audubon Society Nature Odysseys:
212-979-3066

Natural Habitat Adventures:
800-543-8917

Nature Conservancy
  International Trips:
  703-841-5300
World Wildlife Fund:
  800-225-5993

Museum, University, and Scientific Trips
AAAS Travels,
  Betchart Expeditions:
  800-252-4910
American Museum of Natural History
  Discovery Tours:
  800-462-8687
Earthwatch:
  800-776-0188
Harvard Museum of
  Cultural & Natural History:
  617-495-2463
Smithsonian Odyssey Tours:
  800-258-5885
University Research Expeditions
  Program, University of California
  at Berkeley:
  510-642-6586
Contact your alma mater or your local
  university and ask for the alumni
  travel tours office; also check with
  your local zoo or museum.

Photography Trips
Exfoditions:
  310-471-2845
Joseph Van Os Photo Safaris:
  206-463-5383
Photo Adventure Tours:
  800-821-1221
Rocky Mountain School
  of Photography:
  800-394-7677
Voyagers International:
  800-633-0299

Women-Only Trips
Rainbow Adventures:
  800-804-8686
Woodswomen:
  800-279-0555

Senior Trips (ages 50 plus)
Eldertreks:
  800-741-7956
Overseas Adventure Travel:
  800-221-0814

Equestrian Trips
Equitour
  (formerly FITS Equestrian):
  800-666-3487

Expedition Cruises
Marine Expeditions:
  800-263-9147
Quark Expeditions:
  800-356-5699
Society Expeditions:
  800-548-8669
Special Expeditions:
  800-397-3348
Zegrahm Expeditions:
  800-628-8747

Meet-the-People Trips
Earthwatch:
  800-776-0188
Folkways Institute:
  503-658-6600
Global Citizens Network:
  800-644-9292
Global Volunteers:
  800-487-1074

FURTHER READING
The Active Travel Resource Guide, Dan
  Browdy (Ultimate Ventures, 1994)

Adventure Cruising: The Complete Guide to Specialty and Small Ship Cruises, Don Martin and Betty Martin (Pine Cone Press, 1996)

Adventure Travel Abroad, Pat Dickerman (Henry Holt, 1986)

Adventure Vacation Catalogue, Publishers of Specialty Travel Index (Simon & Schuster, 1984)

Adventure Vacations: From Trekking in New Guinea to Swimming in Siberia, Richard Bangs, ed. (John Muir Publications, 1990)

The Big Book of Adventure Travel, James C. Simmons (John Muir Publications, 1997)

Fielding's Guide to the World's Most Dangerous Places, R.W. Pelton (Fielding Worldwide, 1998)

Do's and Taboos around the World, Roger Axtell, ed. (John Wiley & Sons, 1993)

Hiking and Backpacking, Eric Seaborg and Ellen Dudley (Human Kinetics, 1994)

How to Shit in the Woods: An Environmentally Sound Approach to a Lost Art, Kathleen Meyer (Ten Speed Press, 1994)

How to Stay Healthy While Traveling, Bob Young (Blue Pacific Books, 1980)

Insight guidebooks

International Travel Health Guide, Stuart R. Rose (Travel Medicine, 1997)

Lonely Planet guidebooks

The Packing Book: Secrets of the Carry-On Traveler, Judith Gilford (Ten Speed Press, 1996)

The Safe Travel Book, Peter V. Savage (Lexington Books, 1993)

Staying Healthy in Asia, Africa, and Latin America, Dirk G. Schroeder (Moon Publications, 1995)

The Traveler's Handbook, Miranda Haines and Sarah Thorowgood, eds. (Globe Pequot Press, 1997)

Travelers' Medical Resource, William W. Forgey, M.D. (ICS Books, 1990)

The Ultimate Adventure Sourcebook, Paul McMenamin (Turner Publishing, 1992)

Volunteer Vacations: Short-Term Adventures That Will Benefit You and Others, Bill McMillon (Chicago Review Press, 1997)

For more travel books, try these catalogs:

Adventurous Traveler Bookstore: 800-282-3963

Travel Books & Language Center: 800-220-2665

Traveller's Bookstore: 800-755-8728

Also: Check out magazines such as *Outside, Sierra, Backpacker, Audubon;* general travel magazines.

INTERNET SITES OF INTEREST

http://www.adventuretravel.com/ats
Adventure Travel Society:
Lists companies by destination and/or activity; rates these companies as reliable.

http://www.americaoutdoors.com
America Outdoors:
Lists 500-plus national and international adventure travel companies.

http://www.ASTAnet.com
American Society of Travel Agents:
  Lists agents who specialize in
  particular types of trips, including
  adventure travel.

http://www.astmh.org
American Society of Tropical Medicine
  and Hygiene

www.apogeephoto.com
Apogee Photo Directory:
  Gives information on photo tours.

http://www.cdc.gov
Centers for Disease Control and
  Prevention:
  Gives U.S. Public Health Service
  advisories on health, immunizations,
  specific diseases in countries around
  the world.

http://www.oanda.com/cgi-bin/travel
Currency conversions.

http://www.faa.gov
Federal Aviation Administration:
  Rates foreign countries' safety
  oversight of their airlines.

http://www.festivals.com
Festivals around the World:
  Provides a calendar and other
  information.

http://www.istm.org
International Society of Travel
  Medicine:
  Gives a directory of travel medicine
  clinics.

www.lonelyplanet.com
Lonely Planet:
  Posts reports from off-the-beaten-
  path travelers and gives information
  on health risks.

http://expedia.msn.com
Microsoft Expedia:
  Provides current information on
  overseas weather and exchange
  rates.

http://www.mungopark.com
Mungo Park:
  On-line adventure travel zine.

http://travel.state.gov
Overseas Citizens Services Office:
  Provides health and safety tips for
  travelers.

http://www.tripprep.com
Shoreland's Travel Health Online:
  More health and safety information
  for adventure travelers.

http://www.spectrav.com
Specialty Travel Index:
  Lists special-interest tour companies
  by activity and destination.

And try these online travel booking services, which provide information on
carriers, fares, and schedules and allow
you to make reservations online:

Expedia:
  http://expedia.msn.com

Internet Travel Network:
  http://www.itn.net

Preview Travel:
http://www.previewtravel.com

Travelocity:
http://www.travelocity.com

United Connection:
http://flights.ual.com

MEDICAL INFORMATION

Centers for Disease Control:
888-232-3228, 800-311-3435,
404-639-3311. Gives U.S. Public
Health Service advisories on health,
immunizations, specific diseases in
countries around the world.

IAMAT (International Association for
Medical Assistance to Travellers):
716-754-4883. Provides "World
Climate Charts" that include
recommended seasonal clothing and
information on sanitary conditions
of local water, milk, and food by
regions, e.g., East and Northeast
Africa; world immunization charts
and distribution of diseases; world
malaria risk chart and guidelines for
suppressive medication by country.

Medic Alert: 800-432-5378. Provides
bracelet or necklace with phone
number of 24-hour emergency
response center that can dispatch
your medical record to anywhere in
the world.

TRIP AND MEDICAL INSURANCE

Access America:
800-284-8300
International SOS Assistance:
800-523-8930

Mutual of Omaha:
800-228-9792
Travel Assistance International:
800-821-2828
Travel Guard International:
800-826-1300
Travelers:
800-243-3174
TravelSafe:
888-885-7233
Travmed:
800-732-5309
Wallach & Company, Inc.:
800-237-6615
World Care Travel Assistance:
800-253-1877
For more firms, check with the State
Department's Overseas Citizens
Services Office:
202-647-3000

SAFETY AND SECURITY INFORMATION

Association for Safe International Road
Travel:
301-983-5252
Department of State Bureau of
Consular Affairs:
202-647-1488
Department of State Travel Advisories:
202-647-5225; automated fax
service: 202-647-3000
Warnings and safety advice for travel
to specific countries and areas of the
world.
Department of Transportation Travel
Advisory Line:
800-221-0673
Threats to domestic and foreign
transportation systems.

Federal Aviation Administration:
800-322-7873
Rates foreign countries' safety
oversight of their airlines.
International Air Passengers
Association:
800-821-4272 (9 A.M. to 11 A.M.
CST)
Provides information on foreign and
domestic airlines, including types
and average age of planes and
accident rates.
Kroll Travel Watch:
800-824-7502
Provides city-specific reports for
business travelers, including what
parts of town to avoid, safety and
security considerations, getting from
airport to center city, health
considerations, and emergency
phone numbers. Also provides
updates on political unrest, health
emergencies, terrorist activities and
kidnappings, events such as
elections and public holidays, and
safety records for airlines. Issues
safety and stability forecasts.
Superintendent of Documents, U.S.
Government Printing Office:
202-512-1800
Call for health and safety
publications: "A Safe Trip Abroad"
and booklets in the Tips for
Travelers series on different parts
of the world.
U.S. Tour Operators Association:
212-944-5727

ECOTOURISM INFORMATION

Center for Responsible Tourism
415-435-2035
Publishes guides for traveling and
shopping: "Code of Ethics for
Tourists," "Third World: Buy
Critically."
Ecotourism Society:
802-447-2121
Provides "Fact Sheet for Travelers"
with information on conservation,
sustainable development, and
protection of fragile ecosystems.
Partners in Responsible Tourism
510-595-7478
Publishes "Traveler's Code for
Traveling Responsibly—Guidelines
for Individuals"; conducts seminars
on tourism, the environment, and
alternate forms of travel.
World Wildlife Fund
202-293-4800
Publishes "Buyer Beware" booklet
listing banned and endangered-
species products.

CREDIT CARD HOT LINES (TO CALL THE UNITED STATES FROM ABROAD)

American Express:
  301-214-8228
MasterCard:
  303-278-8000
VISA:
  410-581-9994

PASSPORT AND VISA SERVICES

Generations Visa Service:
  800-845-8968
Passport-by-Mail:
  900-225-5674
  (passport renewals)
Trans World Visa Service:
  415-495-5216
U.S. State Department:
  202-663-1225
  (visa information)

A SAMPLING OF TRAVEL PRODUCTS AND CLOTHING CATALOGS

International Travel Outfitters:
  800-355-9375
Magellan's:
  800-962-4943
Sun Precautions:
  800-882-7860
Travel Medicine Inc.:
  800-872-8633
TravelSmith
  800-950-1600

A SAMPLING OF OUTDOOR CLOTHING AND CAMPING PRODUCTS CATALOGS

Campmor:
  800-226-7667
L.L. Bean:
  800-341-4341
Patagonia:
  800-638-6464
REI:
  800-426-4840
Title Nine (for women only):
  800-609-0092

INDEX
